giving
presentations

THE INDUSTRIAL SOCIETY

The Industrial Society stands for changing people's lives. In nearly eighty years of business, the Society has a unique record of transforming organisations by unlocking the potential of their people, bringing unswerving commitment to best practice and tempered by a mission to listen and learn from experience.

The Industrial Society's clear vision of ethics, excellence and learning at work has never been more important. Over 10,000 organisations, including most of the companies that are household names, benefit from corporate Society membership.

The Society works with these, and non-member organisations, in a variety of ways – consultancy, management and skills training, in-house and public courses, information services and multi-media publishing. All this with the single vision – to unlock the potential of people and organisations by promoting ethical standards, excellence and learning at work.

If you would like to know more about the Industrial Society please contact us.

The Industrial Society
48 Bryanston Square
London
W1H 7LN
Telephone 0171 262 2401

The Industrial Society is a Registered Charity No. 290003

how to be
better at....

giving
presentations

Michael Stevens

KOGAN PAGE

The Industrial Society

YOURS TO HAVE AND TO HOLD BUT NOT TO COPY

First published in 1996
Reprinted 1997 (twice), 1998

Kogan Page Limited
120 Pentonville Road
London N1 9JN

© Michael Stevens, 1996

The right of Michael Stevens to be identified as author of this work has been asserted by him in accordance with the Copyright, Design and Patents Act 1988.

British Library Cataloguing in Publication Data
A CIP record for this book is available from the British Library.
ISBN 0 7494 1900 8

Typeset by Photoprint, Torquay, Devon
Printed and bound in Great Britain by Clays Ltd, St Ives plc

CONTENTS

HOW TO BE A BETTER . . . SERIES

Whether you are in a management position or aspiring to one, you are no doubt aware of the increasing need for self-improvement across a wide range of skills.

In recognition of this and sharing their commitment to management development at all levels, Kogan Page and the Industrial Society have joined forces to publish the How to be a Better ... series.

Designed specifically with your needs in mind, the series covers all the core skills you need to make your mark as a high-performing and effective manager.

Enhanced by mini case studies and step-by-step guidance, the books in the series are written by acknowledged experts who impart their advice in a practical way which encourages effective action.

Now you can bring your management skills up to scratch *and* give your career prospects a boost with the How to be a Better ... series!

Titles available are:

How to be Better at Giving Presentations
How to be a Better Problem Solver
How to be a Better Interviewer
How to be a Better Teambuilder
How to be Better at Motivating People
How to be a Better Decision Maker

Forthcoming titles are:

How to be a Better Negotiator
How to be a Better Project Manager
How to be a Better Creative Thinker
How to be a Better Communicator

Available from all good booksellers. For further information on the series, please contact:

Kogan Page, 120 Pentonville Road, London N1 9JN
Tel: 0171 278 0433   Fax: 0171 837 6348

INTRODUCTION

Effective presentation: communicating a message to an audience in a way that produces the desired change in their understanding or opinions.

Communicating with other people is an everyday activity. It comes naturally. We don't consciously think about what we are trying to convey. We don't analyse who we are talking to and what words to use. We don't deliberately change how we talk according to whether it is on the telephone or face-to-face, to one or to several people. We adapt intuitively to the situation. Effective communication is a natural process using skills we all possess.

So why should presentations be any different? For most of us these are not everyday events. We don't know the conventions. We don't have the experience which would let us respond intuitively. We don't have the same confidence that we have in day-to-day situations. The prospect of being in this uncertain situation, where the impression we create may be critical, can torment even the most confident professionals.

The ability to get a message across clearly and convincingly can win business, enhance reputations and help people become more successful generally. Top business leaders rank presentation skills among the most important factors in their success.

Business people make many millions of presentations every day. You don't need to be a great orator to make a successful presentation. You don't even need to be familiar with public speaking. All you need to do is learn how to use your everyday communication skills in this more unusual setting.

This book provides practical advice on how to use your natural ability to become better at giving presentations. It will help you to:

❏ understand what makes a presentation effective;
❏ recognise how you can use your natural abilities to influence an audience;
❏ analyse your audience to identify what they want from your presentation;
❏ use what you know about your audience to give your message more impact;
❏ structure your message so that it is clear and easily understood;
❏ select and design appropriate presentation aids to increase the clarity and impact of your message;
❏ rehearse your presentation to fine-tune your message and your delivery technique;
❏ confidently deliver a presentation which creates interest, enthusiasm and the all important change among members of your audience.

Making presentations has become more important in many people's work. Increased competition has made the ability to influence diverse audiences positively, at work and outside, a critical factor in the success of individuals and their employers. Presentations offer us the opportunity to influence the audiences we are addressing and our career prospects.

Making a presentation is daunting for most people, even seasoned professionals. Self-confidence makes it less threatening and helps you to deliver a presentation that achieves the results you want. This book shows you how to become better at giving presentations by learning how to apply your everyday communication skills.

1

What is a Good Presentation?

There is a fine dividing line between speeches and presentations. On the whole speeches are intended to persuade, entertain or inform, eg political and after-dinner speeches, and are relatively uncommon in a business setting. Presentations have a broader purpose. As well as seeking to persuade they are used to explain ideas, share knowledge and experiences, help the audience to make informed decisions and often to elicit feedback from them.

Presentations come in many forms. Industry conferences, specialist symposia, exhibition seminars, team and departmental presentations, product launches, annual general meetings, press conferences. All seek to achieve something for those involved – the organiser (eg an employer or conference company), the presenter and the audience (especially if they are paying to attend!). A good presentation is one which achieves these objectives by design and not by default. The presentations most likely to achieve their objectives are those delivered with confidence by people who have planned their presentation and are well prepared.

WINNING PRESENTATIONS

A poor presentation of ideas to colleagues at work could result in rejection of a cost-cutting plan and perhaps some loss of face for the presenter. Another presentation might clinch a multi-million pound deal. The stakes vary tremendously but the outcome is always important. If a presentation is worth making it is worth making well.

CASE STUDY

A young executive was asked to speak at short notice at an industry conference in place of her departmental head. She was a relatively new graduate recruit but had spent several months during her course working in Germany with one of the company's business partners. The theme of the conference was 'Business Without Frontiers'. Drawing on her own experience the executive decided to focus on how her employer uses state-of-the-art communications technology when working with its European partners on international projects. This was her first major presentation. She was nervous but prepared carefully and was able to speak confidently about her experience.

Several weeks after the presentation the company heard via the Department of Trade and Industry that a Singaporean engineering group was looking for European partners to help service contracts originating in the Asia Pacific region. The company was one of nearly 80 which responded. It was one of only five invited to Singapore to present detailed proposals. A director of the engineering group had been at the Business Without Frontiers conference. He remembered the young executive's enthusiastic account of working in Germany as part of a pan-European network. It struck a chord.

The case study illustrates some of the many ways in which presentations can deliver benefits. The presenter raised the profile of her company among the audience – enough to secure an opportunity to gain major new business – and her own profile within the company. The audience gained information which, on returning to work, they might have used to improve communications within their own companies.

Often a presentation involves three sets of objectives: those of the presenter, the audience and the organiser (which effectively may be the presenter's employer). The organiser's overall objective is to create a successful conference. Short-term success could be expressed as the number of paying delegates. Generally, though, the organiser would also aim to give delegates value for money because it wants to build a good reputation and secure its long-term success. To give value for money it must create a conference where the presentations meet the audience's needs and expectations. All three sets of objectives are therefore achieved through the audience.

Whatever the message, whatever the occasion, an effective presentation creates a change in the audience eg they become more informed or gain a better understanding of a particular subject. It is through this change that a presentation achieves its objectives.

DELIVERED WITH CONFIDENCE

Inexperienced speakers lacking self-confidence and doing little or no preparation are usually unable to communicate effectively with the audience. Typically they will speak hesitantly and have trouble articulating their words. They may jump from one topic to another without any apparent logic, explaining some ideas in detail and others only superficially. They will speak quickly to avoid long gaps for fear the audience will think they have forgotten what they wanted to say. They may fidget nervously or stand rigidly, staring at some fixed point and avoiding looking directly at the audience.

If a nervous speaker exhibits even some of these signs the impact of the presentation will be reduced dramatically. If there is no eye contact, for example, the audience will feel unconsciously that they are not fully involved in the proceedings. Without any clear structure to what they are hearing they will find it difficult to follow. The absence of pauses will mean they do not have time to digest one idea before they are bombarded by the next.

Having the confidence and conviction to be yourself helps to overcome many of these problems. In everyday situations even people with low self-confidence can usually communicate their ideas effectively. So why not in a formal presentation? One reason is that we assume presentations require a different set of skills. They don't. There is very little difference between how we speak informally to colleagues and how we need to speak to deliver an effective presentation to a large audience.

If you wrote down now how you would like to express a particular idea at a presentation you would think carefully about how you wanted to say it. Almost certainly you would write complete, grammatically correct sentences. That is not how we speak. If we did it would sound unnatural. Listen to people talking. They will often use incomplete sentences. They may ignore all rules of grammar. You can still understand them clearly and it sounds natural. In a presentation we want to sound, and look, as natural and spontaneous as we do in everyday, animated conversation.

There are things which happen naturally when we are talking informally that we can lose in a presentation. We use eye contact, for example, to signal to people that we are going to speak to them and to ensure we have their attention. Then, while we are speaking, we regularly re-establish eye contact to gauge their response, looking for signs that they understand what we are saying. If we sense that they have not understood us we may repeat something, explain it another way or perhaps give an example to illustrate it. We are continually reading the signals from other people and responding to them. Similarly, we use facial expression, gestures and voice intonation automatically to help convey our message. In front of an audience at a presentation we can become rigid with fear and unable to use the skills we apply readily in less formal situations.

Believing that somehow we need to 'perform' differently compounds our nervousness about giving a presentation. Nervousness is a biological response to being in an unusual, uncertain situation. What we need is some way to keep it under control and channel it. To make it serve our purpose. This comes from self-confidence and belief that we can convey our ideas effectively. It translates nervous energy into enthusiasm for our message. The best way to give yourself this confidence is to be well prepared. For any major presentation it is advisable to start preparing weeks in advance.

PLANNED AND WELL PREPARED

If we can communicate clearly in everyday situations without preparation, why do we need to prepare for a presentation? There are two key reasons.

First, during a presentation of 20 minutes or more we will convey a lot of information, much more than is usual in an everyday setting. The audience rarely has an opportunity during a presentation to stop the speaker and ask for explanations. So we must convey our ideas as clearly as possible. We want to give our presentation a structure which is easy to follow and express ideas in ways which the audience can easily understand and digest.

Second, if we are unfamiliar with giving presentations the situation is full of uncertainties. These uncertainties create anxiety which makes it difficult for us to function properly. We have trouble articulating words and cannot think clearly. Preparation helps to take the uncertainty out of the situation. In effect it gives you the confidence to act more naturally.

Let's look at some of these uncertainties. There are basically four components in any presentation. The acronym AM/PM will help you to remember them:

A/M – your *Audience* and the *Medium* through which you reach them

P/M – you, the *Presenter*, and your *Message*

For the inexperienced presenter there are uncertainties in all four areas. What does the audience expect? Will they listen? How will they react to what I am going to say? How should I stand? Do I have to use lots of slides? Should I act authoritatively? What happens if I forget what I want to say? Will they understand what I am talking about? Preparation answers these and many more questions that can trouble the inexperienced presenter (and even some frequent presenters). It also helps you to avoid many of the pitfalls, like the examples in Table 1.1.

Table 1.1 *Some common pitfalls in presentations*

Audience:

❏ You did not understand why people were there – and you did not provide the information they really wanted or needed
❏ You overestimated their knowledge of the subject – and they could not understand what you were talking about

Medium:

❏ You prepared your presentation meticulously, choosing your words carefully, and delivered it word for word – it sounded monotonous and people stopped listening
❏ Your professionally prepared slides looked superb – but as you explained them the audience were more interested in the slides than what you were saying

Presenter:

❏ Anxious to get your message right you kept your eyes fixed on your notes – the audience felt they were being ignored and you did not notice when they became distracted
❏ Worried that people would think you had forgotten what you wanted to say, you avoided pausing – and did not give the audience time to digest one idea before you started explaining the next

Message:

❏ You were not clear about what message you wanted to get across – the audience did not know either
❏ You explained your ideas with excellent examples but they were not relevant to the audience – they lost interest and your message lost its impact

Looking at these examples you will notice that the audience is always the focus of the problem. This is because it is only through the audience that you can achieve the objectives of your presentation. To prepare for any presentation you must start by considering your audience. This is the subject of the next chapter.

KEY POINTS

❑ Preparation helps to give you the confidence to be yourself when you deliver your presentation.

❑ A good presentation achieves its objectives by creating a change among the audience.

❑ There are four elements in any presentation – audience, medium, presenter and message.

❑ Focusing on the needs and expectations of your audience will help you to avoid the common pitfalls.

2

Knowing Your Audience

Achieving the results you want from a presentation relies on knowing your audience. The more you know about them the more control you have in making them listen to, understand and remember your message.

When people attend a presentation they have their own needs and expectations. They are there for a reason even when their attendance is compulsory. The most effective way to get your message across is to deliver it in a way which fulfils their needs and expectations as closely as possible. You want them to listen, so you make your message appealing to them. You want them to understand, so you explain your ideas according to their level of understanding. You want your audience to remember what you say, so you make it strike a chord with them. Sometimes you want to gain agreement, so you emphasise the benefits to the audience. It is not your ideas you are changing, just the way you communicate them. Effectively you are creating a persuasive communication, using the audience's self-interest to achieve your objective.

An audience of more than one is a collection of individuals and not a faceless mass. You want the whole audience to absorb your message so you should appeal to each and every individual. This chapter explains how to analyse your audience and identify which of their characteristics affect how you communicate your message. There are three main steps:

❑ Identify who will be there.
❑ Understand what they expect to gain.

❏ Decide what will encourage them to listen, understand and remember your message.

If you make notes while you are researching your audience you will find them invaluable when preparing your presentation.

WHO WILL BE THERE?

Answering this question can be straightforward or it may require research and careful thought. If you are making a presentation to colleagues or clients, for example, information about them is usually readily available. Identifying who might attend something like an open conference is much more difficult. The amount of information you need about the audience depends largely on how far removed the event is from your day-to-day experience. The more often you have already encountered similar situations the more you will already know, instinctively, about how to respond to the audience to get your message across.

The names of people attending are not important unless you will be addressing people individually or the success of your presentation depends on influencing specific individuals so you need to find out more about them. Generally, though, you should focus on getting an overall feel for the likely make-up of the audience.

A good place to start for any presentation is to consider the occasion. You need to think broadly about the event, its associations and what people will expect to get out of it. This will give you an idea of the range of people who might attend as well as other information you can use to help plan your presentation. This process is useful even when you know who will be attending. Ask yourself:

❏ What type of event is it, eg internal/external, conference, symposium, business pitch?

_____

_____

_____

❑ Who is issuing the invitations?

❑ Is your presentation part of a larger event, eg an exhibition, annual conference, professional symposium?

❑ Where is it being held, eg at home/abroad, internally, conference/exhibition centre, hotel?

❑ Is the event linked to a particular organisation, eg employer, trade body, professional organisation, customer, supplier?

❑ Is there a central theme to the event?

❏ Why are they asking me to speak?
  – What am I doing or involved with that could interest the audience?

  ✐

  _____

  _____

  _____

  – What views or experience do I have that the audience will want to hear?

  ✐

  _____

  _____

  _____

❏ Who else is presenting, eg colleagues, people with the same/different specialisms, competitors?

  ✐

  _____

  _____

  _____

❏ What subjects are they speaking about?

  ✐

  _____

  _____

  _____

❏ Where am I on the agenda?

  ✐

  _____

  _____

  _____

❑   What is the duration of the presentations – mine and any
others?

_____

_____

_____

❑   What is the likely size of my audience?

_____

_____

_____

Armed with this type of information you can start to categorise
the audience. This is purely an exploratory exercise to give you
a feel for your audience and their likely needs and expectations.
Do not let it bias your view. Some groupings which may be
relevant are listed in Table 2.1. You can substitute these with any
you think apply to the subject of your presentation and/or the
occasion.

This type of information becomes relevant when you need to
decide how to convey your message. As a simple example, if all
your audience are female you want to use anecdotes or
examples which are relevant to them and not ones which are
solely applicable to men. Similarly, if your presentation is about
marketing and many of the audience are from finance and
production you want to think about how marketing relates to
these functions.

For some events the organiser is an excellent source of
information. Specialist conference companies, for example, generally design events with a particular audience profile in mind.
They liaise with speakers on the overall theme of their presentations and can tell you the type of delegates they want to attract,
eg their job roles and seniority. If you look at literature

Table 2.1 *Identifying audience characteristics*

- ❑ Male/female ratio
- ❑ Age range
- ❑ Educational range
- ❑ Common interests
- ❑ Economic background
- ❑ Political view
- ❑ Ethnic/racial mix
- ❑ First language
- ❑ Lay people (by background)
- ❑ Professionals (by specialism)
- ❑ Employers/employees, clients/customers existing and prospective (by business sector, job role, rank)
- ❑ Colleagues by rank and department (eg sales, marketing, production, finance)
- ❑ Competitors or rivals

advertising a conference you will often find the following type of information:

- ❑ Details of the conference programme, with the names of speakers and provisional outlines of their presentations.
- ❑ 'Who should attend?', eg 'You will benefit most if you work in sales and marketing, communications, customer service. . .'.

If you analyse presentations in this way you will be much better equipped to prepare effectively. Job titles, for example, indicate people's area and level of expertise. Combined with the business sectors in which they work you can assess their likely level of understanding of your subject. Their likely attitude to the subject may also be apparent.

In some instances, what the audience knows about you, your company or your views may also be important. Your company may be well known for its commitment to fair price trading with Third World suppliers, for example. It is possible, in some circumstances, that members of the audience would resent this fact. Even when the topic is not relevant to your presentation you must be aware that some of the audience could harbour resentment towards you as a representative of your company.

Once you have explored the likely make-up of your audience you can move on to consider their needs and expectations. This will give you further insight into how to deliver an effective presentation.

WHAT DO THEY EXPECT TO GAIN?

You are more likely to get what you want from a presentation if your audience gain something worthwhile too. Knowing why people are attending will help you to decide what they need or expect from your presentation. People usually attend presentations for one or more of the following reasons: to be 'entertained'; attendance is compulsory; they are interested in the subject, or they need information. So your audience may have four different motives for being there.

Often the type of event indicates what motives the audience might have. A free seminar during an exhibition, for example, can attract jaded visitors who want to relax before returning to the bustle of the exhibition. It can also attract people who are seriously interested in learning something. Fee-paying delegates at a conference are also likely to be interested in the subject, even when their employers are paying.

Conference organisers' literature often tells prospective delegates what they can expect to gain by attending, eg:

❏ What are the practical benefits of attending this conference?... Use this opportunity to find out how to:
  - Exploit the opportunities to...
  - Increase your sales impact when...
    Establish the management support for...
  - Equip your sales team to...

With growing pressures at work there are fewer and fewer business people with time to waste attending presentations purely to be 'entertained', but it does happen. The way to grab their attention, and involve them in your presentation, is to

EXERCISE

Imagine you are trying to sell tickets to attend the event at which you will make your presentation. Look at your notes on the type of people you expect to attend and write down the best things they could 'take away' with them. How could they benefit most? This will give you an idea of their possible needs and expectations.

appeal strongly to their self-interest with your opening remarks. Let them know they can get more out of this than 30 minutes light relief. Then keep them interested by making what you say relevant to them. This is the same device used to gain and keep the attention of any audience at a presentation, including those whose attendance is compulsory. Make what is to come sound irresistibly interesting and you have got their attention. Keep feeding them useful information and you will keep their attention.

People may find what you have to say useful in different ways. For example they might use it to:

❑ become more effective at work;
❑ evaluate their options to arrive at a decision;
❑ solve a problem;
❑ become more knowledgeable;
❑ pass on to others;
❑ gain reassurance from knowing their ideas are shared.

These are all needs or desires you can appeal to in your presentation. You should also consider the possibility of hidden agendas. At a company's Annual General Meeting, for example, there may be shareholders who oppose recent strategic developments within the company. They would like others to share their opinions and may take the opportunity to ask questions which highlight their beliefs. In a departmental presentation there may be team members who have personal motives for wanting particular ideas or proposed actions discredited.

From your analysis of the audience you should be able to answer the key question 'What do they want to achieve by being there?' According to the make-up of your audience you may have a range of answers. You can use these, together with other information you have about the audience, to decide the best way to convey your message.

GETTING YOUR IDEAS ACROSS

If what you say meets the audience's needs they are more likely to be interested in, listen to, understand and remember what you say. If what you say offends, is too complex, appears patronising, conflicts with their beliefs, threatens individuals' interests or in any way alienates them you will find it harder to get your message across.

Your first consideration must be getting and keeping your audience's attention. People will tend to be less attentive to what you say when:

❏ they are bored, either because it is not relevant to them, it is relevant but not interesting or they have heard the same thing in an earlier presentation;
❏ you are not giving them the information they expected or need;
❏ they do not understand what you are saying;
❏ they are distracted.

If you have been able to identify what people want to achieve by attending you should easily be able to tailor your message in a way that is relevant, interesting and gives them at least something of what they need or expected. (Techniques for giving your ideas more impact and making them relevant to the audience are examined in the next chapter.)

One of the suggestions made earlier was to find out your position on the agenda. This can be important when an earlier presentation may have covered some of the ground you intend covering. You do not want to deliver the same ideas in the same way. There are two ways you can try to avoid this, although

CASE STUDY

At a conference on rural planning a representative of an airport authority described a strategy his company had used for a proposed major new development. Knowing it would be seeking planning permission, the company decided to open a channel of communication so that likely opposition could be handled on a one-to-one basis. The process began about six months before the planning proposal was submitted. The speaker chose this topic for three main reasons:

❑ Opposition from local residents to new developments is a common problem of which many in the audience would have direct experience.
❑ The company's strategy had been very effective in reducing opposition when the planning proposal was finally submitted.
❑ For the past few months the media had reported daily the battle by protestors, with some success, to stop work on a major new bypass.

In choosing his subject the presenter had been able to identify a common problem of which every member of the audience was aware and most would have direct experience. Most importantly, he was able to offer a practical solution that they might find useful in their own organisation.

neither is guaranteed success. First, you could try to find out the content of the presentation in question. You might try approaching the presenter directly or the event organiser. Second, you could put yourself in the position of the other presenter. Think about the presenter's background, eg job title and employer, and try to imagine how you would convey the ideas in that situation with that experience.

If your presentation is one among others you want it to stand out above the rest. If nothing else it will demonstrate your skill as a communicator but it can also raise your company's profile when your audience includes people from outside. In competitive situations standing out from the crowd can be vital.

Imagine a handful of companies invited to pitch for business. The client will have invited presentations only from companies it knows can deliver a first-class service. Winning the business comes down to the presentations. You need to consider what competitors are offering and try to find significant points of difference which you can highlight as adding extra value to your company's offering. When the selection panel meets to make its decision it will be the outstanding points which are remembered most easily.

When you have people listening you want to ensure they can understand what you are saying. The potential problems are fairly obvious. Your audience may not understand you if:

❑ they cannot hear clearly what you are saying because your voice is too quiet, you do not enunciate clearly or there is excessive background noise;

❑ you use words which are unfamiliar, eg jargon, technical terms;

❑ you do not explain complex ideas or concepts.

If you have prepared and rehearsed adequately you should be able to speak clearly and confidently. Only large venues generally require the use of a microphone and usually this would be arranged by the organiser. If you are involved in the choice of venue avoid sites where there is likely to be distracting background noise. If you are visiting venues remember that you may miss intermittent noise, eg from aircraft, heavy road traffic, people passing.

It is worth considering here what other things might distract your audience. These are important if you are organising your own presentation. They include interruptions, uncomfortable seating or temperatures (too cold or too hot and stuffy), lighting which is too dim or too bright, obstructions which obscure their view of you or your presentation aids, and possibly timing of the presentation too near lunch or the end of the day.

Careful consideration of the language you are going to use is vital. It must be tailored to your audience's level of understanding. You need to know what they know about your subject and their familiarity with the words you might use. Depending on the make-up of the audience this may encompass a wide range of factors, eg nationality or first language, educational and social background, regional colloquialisms, profession, specialism, business sector, terms peculiar to your company. As a general rule you should avoid acronyms, jargon and technical terms unless you know the audience use them regularly.

When members of your audience have different levels of understanding of your subject you have to decide where to pitch it. The dilemma is that if you oversimplify you might sound patronising to some, whereas if you assume too high a level of understanding you will lose others. The biggest danger is actually confusing the less knowledgeable people and losing their interest. Those who know your subject are unlikely to stop listening, particularly if you are using good illustrative examples from your own experience. Selecting examples which the less knowledgeable can identify with personally helps them to understand and you can then pitch your talk slightly higher. Other methods for helping to express your ideas clearly are examined in the next chapter.

Linked to the audience's level of understanding is how they perceive the subject and their likely feelings about your message. For example, look at your analysis of the people attending and ask yourself:

❑ Will they gain or lose by what I say and how?

❑ Do they have preconceived views about this subject, me or my company?

❑ Do our views coincide or differ and by how much?

✎

_____

_____

_____

❑ Do they have a particular axe to grind?

✎

_____

_____

_____

This may bring to light certain obstacles you need to overcome to get your message across effectively. If the audience has misconceptions, for example, you need to correct them in an informative, non-antagonistic way. If you have differing views and acceptance of yours is integral to achieving your objective you will need to back up your views with reasoned explanation. If someone has an axe to grind you must try to pre-empt criticism through your message and still be prepared to handle difficult questions.

Sometimes particularly sensitive issues, like cutbacks and job losses, have to be handled in presentations. Anything which poses a threat to members of the audience can antagonise them. They might try to negate your message with loaded questions or be so galvanised by the threat that they do not listen to your reasoned argument. If your presentation elicits strong reactions of this type you make your task much more difficult. Even seemingly benign issues can elicit a negative reaction. If you presented research findings showing that a particular team working strategy was far more effective than another you risk alienating anyone whose company has invested heavily in the less effective strategy.

You need to consider what might be perceived by the audience as a threat. This is most likely to happen when your ideas:

- ❏ threaten their security or that of their family, friends, or colleagues;
- ❏ infringe on their area of operation;
- ❏ compete for money or space;
- ❏ detract from their prestige or position;
- ❏ damage their reputation or that of colleagues or their organisation;
- ❏ challenge strongly held beliefs, eg political, moral.

Once you are aware of any potential sensitivities you can present your ideas in ways which minimise negative reactions.

You also want to avoid offending your audience. Although political correctness can be taken too far it is simple courtesy not to use material which might be offensive. The most obvious things to avoid are comments which might be offensive on grounds of age, gender, sexual orientation, national or regional origin, religion, politics and membership of minority groups.

Once you 'know' your audience you are in a position to tailor your message specifically for them, which is the subject of the next chapter.

KEY POINTS

- ❏ If you can fulfil audience needs and expectations they are more likely to listen to and remember your message.
- ❏ Try to identify who will be there and what they expect to gain.
- ❏ Imagine yourself in their position and think about how your message will come across to them.

3

PREPARING YOUR TALK

Talking in conversation is so natural that we rarely stop to decide how to convey a message. To achieve the results you want from a presentation you must plan the detail of your message and how best to express it. Analysis of your audience provides guidelines to help you meet their needs. You know broadly what you want to achieve. This chapter shows you how to tie the two together to write a presentation which is clear and convincing. Whatever the subject of your presentation it will help you to:

❑ write objectives to act as guidelines for structuring and developing your message;
❑ gather your ideas to ensure you cover all the important points;
❑ structure your message so that it is easy to follow;
❑ support your ideas so that they are relevant to your audience, clear and have impact;
❑ prepare an outline of your presentation which you can use to rehearse;
❑ identify what questions your talk might prompt the audience to ask;
❑ choose an effective title.

The best way to write a presentation is to start by giving it structure and only then flesh out your ideas. If you try writing it from beginning to end the task will be harder and you risk muddling your message. The starting-point is to be clear about what you want to achieve.

DEFINING YOUR OBJECTIVES

Good presentations are clear and incisive. There is no room for woolly ideas and confused messages. Your presentation needs to be focused, with very clear objectives. These are statements encapsulating what you want to achieve through your presentation. They serve three important functions:

❑ They help you to formulate your message so that it creates the desired effect among the audience.
❑ They help to reduce a complicated message into manageable chunks, making it easier for you to structure your presentation in a way that is easy for your audience to follow and understand.
❑ Achieving them provides a measure of the success of your presentation.

Ask yourself, 'Why am I making this presentation?' Think of it in terms of how you want your audience to have changed after hearing your presentation. This is important. For example, 'To tell people how we manage our dealer network' might answer the question but it is not as useful as 'To have people understand the importance of regular dialogue with dealers'. The second version tells you much more about what information you need to include in your presentation to get the audience response you want. Use words which indicate audience participation, such as believe, understand, agree, do or say, rather than passive words like tell, show, explain or help.

What your audience expects to gain from your presentation (see pages 25–27) together with your own aims will give you a good idea of what areas your objectives should cover. Although you may have one overall aim in mind this may involve more than one objective. Imagine you were presenting a proposal for merging two work groups. Your overall aim might be to gain agreement for the merger. To achieve that aim you might have to demonstrate how efficiency would be improved, the cost benefits and the resulting improved level of customer service. Each of these represents a separate objective which you want to achieve with your presentation.

The more specifically you can state the changes you want to achieve in your audience (ie your objectives) the more effective you can make your presentation. This may involve defining further objectives when you have decided on the structure of your presentation. To check if you have stated your objectives effectively ask yourself:

❑ Is my intention clear?
❑ Does it state what audience response I want?
❑ Is that response measurable?

It is useful to keep a note of your objectives in front of you while you are writing your presentation.

COLLECTING YOUR THOUGHTS

If you are short of time, or confident that you know your subject well, you may be tempted to start outlining your presentation straight away. This is not advisable. You are asking your brain to do three things at once – recall the information, put it in a logical order and state it clearly. However clear your thinking, you risk:

❑ choosing a 'storyline' or structure which is not the simplest or most effective way of getting your ideas across;
❑ excluding important information because you momentarily forget, or because it does not fit into the storyline you have chosen;
❑ not meeting the needs of your audience because you have not included them in the writing process;
❑ not choosing the most important points.

If you first gather all your thoughts on the subject these will help you to decide the best structure to use. Then you can flesh out your ideas. The following method is useful for collecting your thoughts:

❑ Choose a time when you will not be interrupted.
❑ Record all your thoughts on the subject, quickly and randomly.

❏ Do not worry about repetition.
❏ Do not stop to explain, link or justify ideas.
❏ Let the ideas flow and keep writing.
❏ When you have exhausted your ideas put your notes aside.

More ideas inevitably come to mind later but you can simply make a note of these and add them to your list before you start structuring your message.

STRUCTURING YOUR MESSAGE

Brevity and simplicity are key to making a successful presentation, even when addressing a specialist audience.

Keep	KISS is a well-known acronym for making effective presentations:
It	❏ short, because people concentrate best in short bursts
Short and	❏ simple, because the easier it is to follow the more your audience will understand,
Simple	absorb and remember

Even a short and simple message can have a powerful impact. Much of the information conveyed by a good presentation is not expressed directly, it is created in the mind of the audience. Like a short story the presentation draws the audience into the subject and involves them, conjuring images and evoking memories of experiences.

The first step in structuring your presentation is to decide the key points you want to get across. Imagine you are making a presentation on time management. You have identified audience needs and gathered your ideas on the subject. Figure 3.1 illustrates a simple way to show how your ideas relate to audience needs. Once you have identified which of your ideas are most applicable you can decide which key points encapsulate these ideas. In this example you could choose:

❏ Making time.
❏ Time-wasting.

Audience needs   **Subject ideas**

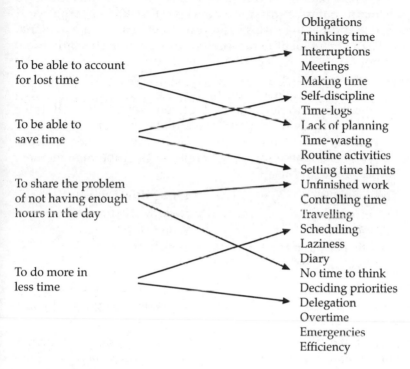

Figure 3.1 *Matching your ideas with audience needs*

❏ Controlling time.
❏ Lack of time.

What you are doing is starting to give a structure to your presentation which will help to satisfy audience needs and breaks down a complex subject into a simple sequence of ideas.

Software is available for outlining and structuring ideas and these facilities are also available in some word processing and presentation graphics software packages. Unless you are familiar with using these facilities you may find it easier to use normal word processing or pen and paper.

Any presentation should have a maximum of only three or four main points. Any more and you risk confusing your audience and having insufficient time to give adequate explanation. If you have identified more points than this check that you have not mistaken explanation (eg interruptions) for a key point (time-wasting). What you need is the widest 'umbrella' ideas under which the others could fit.

The next step is to flesh out each of your key points with three or four main ideas from your notes that you want to cover in your presentation. Remember to bear in mind audience needs when you select these topics. Continuing the time management example you could use:

Time-wasting
Interruptions
Laziness
Lack of planning

Controlling time
Deciding priorities
Scheduling
Self-discipline

Making time
Delegation
Travelling
Setting time limits

Lack of time
Unfinished work
No time to think
Overtime

The final step is to decide the best order to present your key points. Usually there will be a 'natural' order which you (and subsequently your audience) recognise as the most logical way of explaining your subject. A structure common in the commercial, technical and scientific worlds is the statement of a problem followed by the description of a solution, eg:

The problem		The solution
Lack of time	$\longrightarrow$	Making time
Time-wasting	$\longrightarrow$	Controlling time

Variations of this type of structure include asking a question and answering it, or highlighting a need and fulfilling it. Other types of natural order may be determined by importance or size, temporal order, or by cause and effect. If there is a natural order use it. Your audience will find it easier to follow. Once you have decided on the order you can start to flesh out your ideas.

GIVING YOUR IDEAS IMPACT

Now is the time to start thinking about how best to convey your ideas. You are not writing your presentation at this stage but deciding how you will convey your main points. You want to do this in a way which will:

❑ keep the audience's attention, sparking interest and enthusiasm;
❑ involve the audience by making your ideas personally relevant to them;
❑ make what you say memorable;
❑ persuade your audience, when necessary.

An audience is stirred by ideas delivered with impact. They are aroused and mentally prepared to think about the significance of what you are saying and absorb your message. A wide variety of methods can be used to give ideas impact. A selection of these is shown in Table 3.1. Two other ways of helping to convey ideas with impact are visual and other presentation aids and your voice and body language. These are covered in later chapters.

Using any of these methods to best effect depends on knowing your audience. The following sections illustrate how some of them can be used to keep your audience's attention,

Table 3.1 *Devices used to convey ideas with impact*

Analogy	Facts
Anecdote	Humour
Anticlimax	Metaphor
Curiosity	Narrative
Definition	Opinion
Description	Questions
Emotion	Quotations
Exaggeration	Repetition
Example	Statistics
Explanation	Understatement

give your ideas impact and make them memorable and, when necessary, persuade your audience.

Keeping their attention

We all become bored and distracted watching and hearing something which is of no interest. You must *make* your audience listen and keep listening. There are many ways of doing this. First, you need to grab people's attention. You could appeal to their curiosity, for example, with an opening line such as 'I'm going to tell you how you can do twice as much in half the time ... *without* exerting yourself'. They will listen if you promise something which appeals to them. Continue to provide interesting ideas which fulfil that promise and they will keep listening. You could give an example which strikes a chord with the audience, such as the amount of time the average manager wastes fielding inessential telephone calls on his direct line.

Anecdotes are another way of generating interest. For example: 'I remember as a schoolboy trying to trade with my parents – washing the car, tidying my room, even my pocket money – just so that I could stay up to watch a late-night boxing match. We all learn very early in life where the balance of power lies in supply and demand.'

When you think your audience might be getting restless you could frighten them to attention with an alarming statistic. Playwrights learn how to sustain audience attention by using moments of drama to create tension. Just before this has ebbed away they introduce another gripping scene. And so on until they deliver the ultimate climax (or sometimes anticlimax). You do not need a dramatist's skill to do this in a presentation. Just be aware that your audience's attention will begin to flag, sometimes after only a couple of minutes, if you do not regularly spark their interest.

Another device used to keep an audience alert, particularly smaller groups, is to ask for feedback. For example, you could ask how, in their experience, a particular problem arises. Any device which demands a response and gets them thinking about your topic from their viewpoint will help you to keep their minds focused on what you are saying. Rhetorical questions serve the same purpose. You pose a question and pause before giving your answer. The question focuses the audience's attention and automatically they start to think up their own answers.

A mistake some people make is to think that the more detailed information they give the more interested and attentive the audience will be. This is not true. Information takes time and effort to digest. Give people too much and you will soon wear them down. It is much better to be crisp and concise, giving little chunks of information communicated in a way which brings the subject alive for the audience.

Make it memorable

Human memory is basically a very sophisticated filing system. Before we can store information in our memory we need to digest it, analysing where it should be 'filed'. Information which is easier to 'file' is therefore easier to remember. The larger the volume of information the more time it takes to analyse and file.

If you convey an idea in a way that the audience can identify with they will find it easier to remember. There are two reasons. First, when they recognise the similarities between your idea and their experience they are recalling that experience from memory, ie they have found the relevant 'file'. Adding new information is therefore much easier. Second, since some of the information in your idea is already stored in their memory they have less additional information to memorise. Ideas with which they can identify personally therefore involve them more, because they automatically recall the common experience, and are memorised with less effort. If you also make the information useful to the audience they have a reason to remember it, as illustrated by the case study.

Repetition can be used to reinforce a key point but try to illustrate it using different common experiences. If you can do this you encourage the audience to remember the same point in two different ways, ie they are filing the same idea in two or

CASE STUDY

At a conference on improving marketing performance a manager spoke about his company's implementation of a new computer system. He had talked about establishing user requirements and then the experience of meeting different suppliers. Before explaining how the company decided which system to buy he gave the audience a tip: 'Ignore all the bells and whistles you will be shown. Focus on the key things you want to achieve'. Then he went on to describe the selection criteria the company had used. That simple tip struck a chord with the audience. It answered a question with which everyone could identify – 'How do you evaluate the widely differing systems available?' It also encapsulated a key point of the presentation.

more separate parts of their mental filing system. If you labour a point too much, however, your audience will switch off.

Audience analysis provides clues to common experiences, needs and concerns which you can use to convey your main points. Even with subjects beyond their experience there should be elements of common understanding from their professional or personal lives. The more you can bring your key points alive – with vivid examples, anecdotes, analogies and other links to common experiences – the more information your audience are likely to absorb and remember.

Persuading your audience

Persuasion is not the same as manipulation. Persuading the audience is a process of helping them to see your ideas in a positive way. You can do this either by logical argument, presenting one or both sides, or by satisfying audience needs and desires.

You should be aware of any likely opposition from analysing your audience. Choosing carefully how you express your ideas can help you to overcome this opposition. Imagine you are telling a company salesforce about a proposal to increase their number by 20 per cent and reduce the size of individual sales areas. The purpose is to give better market coverage, increase customer satisfaction and boost profits. The sales people, knowing the basic proposal, come to the presentation anxious that their commission is threatened. You could use logical argument to overcome their opposition. This must always be based soundly on fact. In this case you could present the facts in various ways, eg:

❑ Quote statistical evidence to show that smaller sales areas will yield the same turnover, and commission, as the current sized areas.
❑ Give an example of projected sales in one of the newly defined areas.
❑ Describe a parallel situation in which the sales people benefited as well as the company.

When you are trying to persuade by logical argument there is a temptation to bombard people with facts to reinforce it. This is generally counterproductive. If you do need to give heavy-weight statistics and other supporting evidence you should provide it in a written document handed out at the end of your presentation. Keep your presentation crisp and concise other-wise you will dilute the force of your argument.

Deciding whether to present just your side of an argument or to incorporate answers to the counter-argument depends on who is in your audience. Table 3.2 gives some hints on how to decide which approach to use. If you choose to present one side

Table 3.2 *Deciding whether to present one or both sides of an argument*

One side when	Both sides when
Most are in favour	Most are opposed
Subordinates rely on you for guidance	Superiors will want the full picture
They have to make a decision on the spot	The counter-argument has been or is going to be made known

of an argument you still need to prepare notes on the counter-argument. This will equip you to answer any questions from your audience when you deliver your presentation.

Motivating people to accept an argument by dangling a carrot can be effective provided the carrots are real and tangible. Audience analysis will tell you what needs and desires might motivate your audience. If you have a carrot which appeals to them you can use it to persuade. For example, imagine your company had made a takeover bid for another business and you are appealing to its shareholders. You need to present an argument which appeals to their needs and desires. There are many ways of doing this. For example, depending on the situation, you could:

❑ appeal to greed, with an offer they cannot refuse;
❑ guarantee their independence, by confirming that there will be no interference in the company if the takeover is successful;
❑ appeal to their sense of adventure, if yours is a company with big ideas.

Other needs and desires you can appeal to include ambition, approval, belonging, loyalty, power, pride, recognition, reward, security and self-respect.

The motivation technique needs to be used with caution because in some situations it may be ineffective and can even antagonise your audience. Your superiors, for example, might think you arrogant if you claim to know what is in their best interests. It is also a more subtle method of persuasion than logical argument and may not work if there is a strong counter-argument. In some situations, however, this subtlety can work for you. In a business pitch, for example, the final choice may come down to the people and the organisation the client would like to work with. This can be turned to advantage. Imagine the client company is conservative and research shows that other businesses working for them are also conservative. A presentation from a company which is perceived to be conservative will stand more chance of winning the business than one which comes across as being more adventurous.

If you are speaking on behalf of, or for, someone else (like a colleague or employer) remember that you may have to obtain approval of what you intend to say. This is especially important if you are speaking at an open event about company operations. The inadvertent release of sensitive information can be disastrous. It can wipe out any commercial advantage to be gained from recent developments in the company as well as give advantage to other businesses. Careers have also been destroyed by unguarded comments.

As you identify ways to convey your main points you can check how effective they are likely to be by asking yourself:

- ❑ Is it true to the point I want to make?
- ❑ Will the whole audience be able to identify with it?
- ❑ Is it clearly stated?
- ❑ Is it easy to understand?

Do not worry if you cannot think of good ways to convey all your points, or you are not satisfied with some you have chosen. As you start to put them together in an outline you will often find that other ideas come to mind. Remember also that you can use presentation aids (covered in the next chapter) to help convey your ideas.

OUTLINING YOUR PRESENTATION

By this stage you have a list of points you want to cover and notes on how you could convey them. The process of outlining ties these two together into a single storyline and provides a script you can use to rehearse.

Like a good story a presentation needs a beginning, middle and end. The maxim you should follow is:

1. Tell them what you are going to tell them.
2. Tell them
3. Tell them what you have told them.

This might sound simplistic but it works very well and is used widely by experienced presenters. With your opening remarks you are setting the scene. People want to know what to expect and by telling them you are making it easier for them to absorb what you say later. With your closing remarks you are summarising your entire message and consolidating the mental picture you have created during your talk. The peak of concentration for an audience in a presentation is usually over after the first minute or so, with an increase in interest again when they realise the end is near. Using your introduction to preview your message and your conclusion to review it takes advantage of these two peaks of audience attention.

A strong opening does a lot to help carry your audience through the remainder of your presentation. Audience attention is highest at this point and you can spread this benefit by telling them how your talk is structured, ie giving an overview of your key points. Throughout your talk the audience will then have a framework into which they can fit everything you say. Try to open with an example, anecdote or other illustrative device which encapsulates your message.

The body of your presentation will follow the structure you determined earlier and use the various devices you have chosen to give impact to your key points.

Your closing lines will convey more or less the same message as your opening but expressed in a different way. Try to make it climactic, such as a call to action, instilling in the audience a sense of personal empowerment or achievement. Make them feel you have given them something important to take away with them. Again, use an anecdote, example or other device to help them identify with it. Depending on the event, at this point you might be expected or want to invite questions and comments. This is an opportunity to further influence the audience. More preparation is required and this is examined later in this chapter.

Your introduction and conclusion serve particularly important functions and need to be thought out very carefully. Some tips on formulating them are shown in Table 3.3.

Text to be read and text to be spoken are quite different. We have all heard people reading from prepared text and noticed how lifeless and unnatural it can sound. Sometimes material has to be prepared this way. Official statements read on television or radio, for example, are often written for publication rather than

Table 3.3 *Tips on formulating your introduction and conclusion*

Your introduction should	Your conclusion should
❏ Get audience attention and focus it on your theme	❏ Review what you have said with a summary or an example which ties everything together (*never* introduce new points)
❏ Give them a taste of what is to come	
❏ Tell them the content and structure of your presentation	❏ Be memorable
	❏ State or imply what you expect your audience to do or believe, know, etc as a result of your talk

oral delivery. A presentation, even if delivered from a full script, should sound natural and therefore has to be written in a conversational style. In addition, it should be written in *your* conversational style. If you attempt to change your style you will be suppressing your own personality. When you deliver your presentation you would lose any natural enthusiasm and spontaneity. The following method of outlining your presentation is useful because it encourages you to use your own natural conversational style:

❏ Put your key points in order, together with your notes on how you want to convey them.
❏ Take each one in turn and describe it to an imaginary friend sat in front of you.
❏ Include the illustrative devices you have chosen at the appropriate places.
❏ Keep your explanation as brief as possible.
❏ Try to do this spontaneously, noting down the actual words and phrases you think of as you describe your ideas to the imaginary friend.
❏ Do not stop to deliberate or correct, just concentrate on conveying your ideas.
❏ When you pause for thought indicate it in your notes (eg by long dashes).

What you end up with is closer to everyday conversation than if you had simply written an explanation of your ideas. There may be pauses, repetition, incomplete sentences, short snappy explanations and contractions such as 'we'd' rather than 'we did'. On the page this may look strange but when read aloud it will sound natural.

The next step is to edit and check your notes to ensure your explanation matches the audience's level of understanding. Avoid long and uncommon words, jargon and technical terms without explanation, ambiguity and vague words like 'excessive' and 'somewhat'. Editing should streamline your notes but not dramatically change the style or structure. For example, check that you have linked successive points in a way that tells the audience how they are related. Give summaries between main points if the subject is complex. Use links such as 'first', 'as a result', 'this led to', while avoiding repeated use of words or phrases like 'next', 'now', 'and so', 'also', and 'therefore'. You may find that, having given expression to your ideas, you want to rearrange some of your points to make them clearer.

You want your presentation to be crisp and concise. If you need to convey detailed information it is best to prepare a written document to give out at the end of your presentation. Simply deliver the key point during your talk and say that more detailed information is available in the handout.

You need to decide whether you want to deliver your presentation from notes or from a full script. In making this decision remember that you will be rehearsing so you will become familiar with the ideas you want to communicate. It can be more difficult, and requires just as much rehearsal, to deliver effectively from a full script. Sometimes you will have to provide a script of your talk, either to the organisers in advance or to delegates after your presentation. So you have four options at this stage: prepare notes to deliver your talk, prepare the notes and a script to be read, prepare a script to speak from, prepare one script to speak from and one to be read.

When you prepare a script to deliver your talk you want to retain the conversational style. As you work through your edited notes speak the words to yourself. Avoid restructuring sentences simply because they are ungrammatical. Avoid the temptation to elaborate or merge sentences. Keep them short and snappy. Rehearsal will help you to fine-tune your script and ensure that it sounds natural when read aloud.

A written script to be given to the audience does not have to be word for word the same as your talk. However, it should be as close as possible, conveying the same ideas, in the same order and using the same descriptive devices. It is a straightforward writing task to turn your notes into a document that reads well. There is a temptation to elaborate your ideas because it is a written document. Don't. The content should be the same as your presentation. If you want to provide additional information give it in a separate part of the document.

If you want to deliver your talk from notes these need to trigger recall of what you want to say. Once you have rehearsed your presentation it is surprising how little information you need as a trigger. When you start rehearsing, however, you will probably need to use your full set of notes. Then, once you are familiar with the content, you can edit these down to bullet points. Use at least one card for each key point. You may need more if there are several lesser points under each heading. Try to ensure that each card represents approximately the same amount of speaking time. This will help you keep your talk on track. Each bullet point should be as short as possible. You will have to decide during rehearsal what words work best as a trigger for you. When you prepare your final notes use a clear typeface and large print.

Whether you are using notes or a full script you may find during rehearsal that you need to shorten your talk to fit into the allotted time.

WHAT QUESTIONS MIGHT PEOPLE ASK?

Now is a good time to start thinking about what type of questions people might ask you as a result of your presentation. Question and answer sessions are not always on the agenda but they can be useful. It gives you an opportunity to ensure people have understood your message and to provide any additional information they want. Remember that satisfying audience needs helps you to achieve your objectives, so it is important to be well prepared to answer questions.

If you intend taking questions tell the audience early in your presentation that you will be happy to answer questions at the appropriate time. Some conference speakers also make themselves available during coffee breaks to answer questions individually.

You cannot cover every eventuality but you can predict what people are likely to ask. It depends largely on audience needs and expectations and how well you satisfy these in your presentation. For example, ask yourself:

❏ Is anything in my talk contentious?

_____

_____

_____

❏ Are there aspects of the subject about which people might want to know more?

_____

_____

_____

❏ Do I cite anonymous examples that people might want named?

_____

_____

_____

❑ Have I had to omit any significant information because of time limitations?

✎

❑ Have I deliberately omitted certain information?

✎

❑ Have I made claims which might need further proof?

✎

❑ Is there anything in my talk which might require further explanation?

✎

❑ Does anyone in the audience have an axe to grind?

✎

Put yourself in the audience's position and make a note of anything in, or omitted from, your talk which could elicit a question. If you are using a script ask a friend or colleague to read it and say, 'Tell me what I've left out'. If you are speaking from notes you can ask someone to sit in on your rehearsal. This also gives you the opportunity to practise answering questions spontaneously.

As you think of questions people might ask, make a note of what you could say in response. Tips on responding to questions are given in Chapter 5 (page 76).

CHOOSING AN EFFECTIVE TITLE

The importance of a presentation title depends on how significant a role it will serve. When you want to encourage people to attend it can be very useful. You can use it to grab their attention and make them eager to find out more. In other situations, such as routine internal presentations where attendance is compulsory, a talk may not be given a formal title. It could be regarded as superfluous dressing. Even in these situations, however, a good title can heighten interest and focus expectations. Like your opening remarks it helps to prepare people for what is to come. You will have to decide whether or not it is appropriate to use a title for a particular presentation.

If you are coining a title for your presentation it is vital that it captures the essence of your message. If your title is in any way misleading it will create expectations that your presentation does not fulfil. As a result some people may be disappointed.

Here are three titles given to real presentations:

10 Steps To A Smarter Database

Customer Relationship Marketing – Lessons Learnt

Identifying and Monitoring the Disparate Needs and Wants of A Complex Customer Base in a Market Characterised by Ever Shorter Product and Customer Lifecycles

All three tell you what you could expect to learn from the presentations. The third tells you in considerable detail. Despite that detail, however, it does not create a clear mental picture of what the presentation is about. The title is often the first contact people have with your presentation and it could be the last. First impressions count. The title should give your audience an exciting glimpse of what is to come and crystallise their thoughts on the subject. If you cannot encapsulate the subject in a few words, perhaps because you are covering just a few aspects of a wide-ranging subject, use a subtitle to define a more generalised title. Here is another real example:

Towards Zero Defections: Maximising Customer Retention by Analysing the Relative Impact of the Critical Soft Factors That Secure Long-Term Loyalty

Once you have read the full title the snappy term 'Towards Zero Defections' serves as an easy reminder of what to expect. In general an effective title should:

❏ be brief (try to keep to five or less words);
❏ arouse audience interest;
❏ encapsulate your message;
❏ be meaningful in its own right.

While planning your talk you may have decided that you need to use presentation aids as support. These are examined in the next chapter. If you are not using any aids you can start rehearsing your presentation, which is covered in Chapter 5.

KEY POINTS

❏ Clarify your objectives in terms of how you want the audience to change as a result of your presentation.
❏ Collect all your ideas before structuring your talk.
❏ Select the three or four key points you want to convey and three or four sub-headings for each one.
❏ Use a mix of the devices available to give your ideas impact.
❏ Use your introduction to preview and your conclusion to summarise your message.

4

PRESENTATION AIDS

Sometimes spoken words alone are not the most effective way of conveying information. One research study showed that visual aids, the most commonly used presentation aid, can increase a presenter's persuasiveness by 43 per cent. Generally only a small proportion of what a presenter says is remembered. Presentation aids can increase significantly the amount of information retained by an audience. This chapter will help you to:

❏ understand the features of a good presentation aid;
❏ recognise the wide range of support available;
❏ select the most effective aid for the job;
❏ understand how to integrate them in your presentation.

The proper use of presentation aids is to communicate information more effectively than you can do just by speaking. If you use them inappropriately they will have a detrimental effect on your presentation.

BENEFITS AND DRAWBACKS

Developments in technology have encouraged people to make greater use of support for presentations. Sophisticated presentation graphics software has become more accessible and user-friendly, encouraging the use of slides or computer graphics when often there is no sound reason. Advances in projection equipment, lighting and other technologies have given rise to events which rely more heavily on spectacle. It is tempting to think that using state-of-the-art support intrinsically improves the quality of a presentation. Any supporting aids only add value if they have specific functions which cannot be better served by speaking.

Some people have a tendency to use too many visual aids. One presentation software package will automatically rearrange bullet points into any one of 22 different layouts! This encourages people to look for impressive ways to display information when visual representation may not be required at all.

Visual aids are the most popular form of presentation support. They include anything which can be used to convey information visually, such as slides and computer-generated graphics, flip charts, chalkboards, overhead projection and video. The best type of visual aid is one which capitalises on the visual image. A simple example is presenting rows of figures as a graph or pie chart to show clearly the meaning of the figures. All too often visual aids are used inappropriately, conveying content rather than meaning. .

There are potentially many advantages to presenting information visually:

❑ The audience can absorb information in a way and at a rate which suits them.

❑ It provides a refreshing change from just listening and can grab audience attention.

❑ It is easier to understand complex information (eg relationships, procedures and summaries) when it is represented visually.

❑ Pictures can stimulate the imagination instantly and more easily than words, increasing audience involvement.

❑ Images can trigger strong emotional responses and generate a particular mood among the audience.

❑ Images can convey information more concisely ('a picture is worth a thousand words').

❑ Information presented visually is remembered for a longer time.

Used appropriately visual aids can alter audience mood, get their attention, help them understand and remember your key points and support and reinforce your message. When used for the wrong reasons or in the wrong way they serve no useful purpose and can even detract from your presentation. For example, they can:

❑ distract the audience from your message;
❑ distract you from your purpose, eg by having to write, draw, operate equipment;
❑ mislead the audience if they are not appropriate;
❑ confuse the audience if they are not well designed;
❑ add unnecessary complexity to your presentation.

The same drawbacks can apply to all presentation aids when they are used inappropriately. Anything you use to support what you say should be:

❑ the best method available to convey the idea;
❑ an accurate representation of the idea;
❑ designed to capitalise on the particular benefits of the method, eg visual images in visual aids;
❑ easy to understand;
❑ used effectively during the presentation.

You are the main feature of your presentation. Projecting your enthusiasm and personality is the most powerful way of influencing your audience. If you decide you must use additional support select your methods carefully. Do not opt automatically for the most common methods because the choice is much wider and each offers a different mix of benefits.

TYPES OF PRESENTATION AID

Anything is permissible in supporting your presentation if it serves your purpose. Appearing out of a stage trapdoor, a slapstick comedy sketch, telephones ringing on the podium. If you can think of a way to get an idea across and produce exactly the audience reaction you want there is nothing to stop you using it. The nature of most business presentations will call for

Table 4.1 *Some methods of supporting a presentation*

Slides	Chalkboards/whiteboards
Computer-generated graphics	Flip charts
Audio recordings	Handouts
Video and film	Demonstrations
Storyboards	Props
Displays or exhibits	An audience plant
Overhead projection	Stunts
Video conference links	

more routine types of support but start with an open, anything-goes frame of mind. Then your choice of support is more likely to be guided by effectiveness rather than convention. Today's professionally staged business presentations are slick affairs but sometimes lack imagination. Use presentation aids innovatively and you can create additional impact.

Some of the many methods for supporting presentations are shown in Table 4.1. Each of these has qualities which makes it suitable for use in particular circumstances. Some methods are more suited than others to particular lighting conditions, for example, and different sizes of audience or venue. Some allow images to be created in front of the audience (eg flip charts) and some can incorporate up-to-the-minute data in graphic form (computer-generated graphics). There is almost unlimited scope for supporting a presentation.

Presentation aids can have a powerful impact on the audience. If you choose an inappropriate method of support that impact can be negative. Deciding which aids to use, if any, therefore requires as much care as you take in preparing your spoken message.

DECIDING WHAT SUPPORT YOU NEED

Any support aids you use are an integral part of your presentation and you should select them during the writing process. Consider whether particular ideas could be conveyed more effectively using something to supplement or instead of your spoken words. If you decide you need some support device ask yourself:

❑ What type of help or support do I need to get this idea across effectively?
❑ Which is the best aid to provide that support?
❑ What is the most effective design for the aid I have chosen?

What form of support?

It is usually quite obvious from the nature of the information you want to communicate what function you want the aid to serve. For example, you may want to:

❑ *explain* a concept, or the consequences of an event;
❑ *reinforce* key points, radical ideas or proposals;
❑ *clarify* complex data, relationships or procedures;
❑ *define* a situation, or the scope of a problem;
❑ *prove* a radical statement, or a conclusion;
❑ *generate* a mood to make the audience more receptive to a particular idea.

If you decide first what function you want the aid to serve it helps you to identify an appropriate method. Take the subject of world famine as an example. There are many possibilities for communicating relevant information. For example, you could:

❑ define the problem with statistics on food shortages or resulting mortality rates;
❑ explain the consequences of malnutrition;
❑ clarify the causes of regional food shortages;
❑ generate a particular mood by showing the extent of Western food mountains alongside the suffering of Third World children.

The type of support you need will depend on the main points you want to get across. A fund-raiser for famine relief, for example, might want to generate sympathy for the plight of Third World children and guilt about food mountains in the

Western world. A representative of a pharmaceuticals company may be more inclined to concentrate on the consequences of malnutrition. Decide first what form of support you need, then you will be able to decide the most appropriate aid to fulfil that function.

What type of aid?

Each type of presentation aid has qualities which make it suited to a particular range of uses. The intended function of the aid helps to decide which type you need. They differ in the type of information they are best suited to communicating and the 'texture' of the communication.

Slides are ideally suited to giving graphic form to sets of figures and displaying mood-altering pictures. Computer-generated graphics can also show vividly how market share, profit and other data are changing over time. Flip charts can be used to reveal step-by-step a sequence of events or ideas, such as the solution of a problem or the development of an argument. Sound recordings, video conferencing, film and video bring the outside world into the presentation. Handouts can go beyond traditional documents supporting a presentation to include such things as product samples and cartoon postcards on seats (a simple way of giving the audience a humorous insight into what is to come). An audience 'plant' can help you present two sides of an argument, by raising objections which you answer, or lead your presentation in a new direction by asking you a question.

You should also consider the effect of pre-prepared aids (eg slides) versus those created in front of your audience (written, drawn or staged). Pre-prepared aids like slides can add prestige to a presentation if they look professional. On the other hand something produced on-the-spot creates a more intimate atmosphere and helps to involve the audience.

Handouts, distributed after you have spoken, can be a valuable extension of your presentation. Even if you have no additional information to give the audience, a hard copy summary of your talk, including copies of slides, can be a useful reminder for the audience.

Sometimes circumstances may preclude you from using particular aids. Factors such as audience size, lighting conditions, availability of equipment and time or budget to prepare materials can all limit your choice. Audience size and lighting conditions, for example, dictate the types of projection equipment which can provide a picture of appropriate size and clarity. Unless the event is being staged by a production company, which will provide audiovisual equipment appropriate to the venue, you should check that what you have in mind is available and suitable for your purpose.

If you are satisfied that you can use the aid you have chosen, the next step is to design it to be as effective as possible.

Designing your aid

Even if you intend using aids which are already available you should check that they are well designed and of good quality. Poorly designed slides or other aids will lessen the impact of your message even in an otherwise excellent presentation. Be sure to preview carefully any materials you are using from an outside source.

Try to capitalise on the best features of the support device you have chosen. The clearest example is visual aids, which should be used for their ability to convey information using shape and form. Slides can be used effectively to provide the audience with a written summary of key points but these must be succinct. The most potent visual aids are those which give form and meaning to your message using graphics or other visual elements.

Figures 4.1 and 4.2 illustrate alternative ways of conveying an idea using slides. Figure 4.1 contains more information but the concept of a communication barrier is conveyed with much more impact in Figure 4.2. Using this, the details could be explained verbally or conveyed with more slides or other aids. In general the acronym KISS (Keep It Short and Simple) applies to presentation aids as well as your spoken words. It is better to use several simple aids which have high impact than to dilute

The PRESENTER'S MESSAGE is conveyed through:	. . . but there can be a COMMUNICATION BARRIER created by:	. . . and THE AUDIENCE HAS NEEDS too, for:
❏ words	❏ lack of explanation	❏ specific information
❏ images	❏ distractions	❏ understanding
❏ structure	❏ disinterest	❏ involvement
❏ emphasis	❏ misinterpretation	❏ recognition
❏ gesture	❏ poor articulation	❏ security

Figure 4.1 *A badly designed slide*

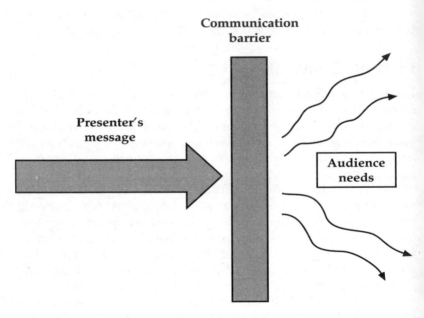

Figure 4.2 *Using shape and form to convey meaning*

your message with detail. With the exception of photographs, visual aids generally should be:

❏ simple, with detail large enough to be seen by the most distant members of the audience;

❑ uncluttered and crisp-looking, with blank spaces making important features stand out;

❑ as visual as possible, with key words or phrases, if necessary, rather than sentences.

The same principles apply to aids created in front of your audience. If you intend using a flip chart, for example, plan what you intend to write or draw, bearing in mind the impact it will have on the audience. If using props or 'stunts' do not embellish them with unnecessary activity. Printed information in handouts should be well structured and clearly laid out. Remember to use the same structure and key words or phrases as in your talk.

There are many specialist slide production companies employing professional designers who will create slides to a brief. Or they can produce slides you have designed using one of the popular presentation graphics software packages. Leading software packages have become very sophisticated and easier to use. They provide tips on design and highlight potential design faults to help you achieve maximum impact. It is vital to remember, however, that if the concept is ill-conceived no amount of design expertise will create a slide which has the impact you want to achieve.

The final hurdle in getting the best out of whatever aids you select is to use them effectively during your presentation.

USING PRESENTATION AIDS

One of the major problems with presentation aids is that they can interrupt the flow of a presentation and disrupt the rapport you have built up with your audience. They also make delivering the presentation more complicated, eg by having to draw or operate equipment. What you say should be the focus of your presentation with the aids supporting *you*.

Visual aids in particular grab audience attention away from the presenter and can be a powerful distraction from your message. Sometimes a presenter will show a slide of key points and then talk the audience through them. Audience attention focuses on the slide, they read it and ignore what the presenter is saying. Because they read faster than the presenter speaks they finish sooner and then have no reason to listen to a recital of what they have read. The slide loses its purpose and the presenter loses audience attention.

Printed handouts, if distributed before your presentation, can be the most distracting. At least some of the audience will scan the material at the very time you want their full attention – when you make your opening remarks.

Using an autocue can also cause problems. It enables you to maintain eye contact with the audience while reading your speech. If you think about how we talk to people in everyday situations you will recognise this is unnatural. We tend to look away from people frequently when we talk to them.

The following guidelines will help you to use presentation aids effectively.

❑ If you intend using equipment make sure it is available, working on the day and you know how to operate it.

❑ With visual aids make your point and then introduce the aid. Put it on screen and look at it with the audience. Keep it on screen long enough for the audience to absorb the information and then remove it. Re-establish eye contact and continue your talk. Only if absolutely necessary should you talk while it is on screen. Even then wait a few seconds while the audience scan the aid, face the audience again and make your comment, keeping it short.

❑ If you are using a flip chart or overhead projector to build up an overall picture of something like a process, either cover or remove what you have written or drawn before you resume talking. Then display it again once you have made your next point and want to add it to the display. When you are writing or drawing make it large enough for all to see, keep it simple and legible and write or draw quickly. With any visual aid remember always to re-establish eye contact with the audience before resuming your talk.

❏ Only distribute written information in handouts before your presentation if it is absolutely necessary. If it is, try to let the audience have it well before you begin your presentation so that they can read it. If you are going to talk the audience through the material, and you have distributed the handout before the presentation day, make sure you have additional copies for everyone on the day.

❏ If you are using an autocue look away from the audience frequently, pausing as you do so, to create a more natural interaction. You can use dummy notes for this purpose. Even if you do not, imagine you need to scan your notes for your next point. This will help you with eye contact and to pause in a natural way.

❏ Finally, make sure you have all your aids with you on the day, slides are in the right order, and so on.

Selected carefully, designed well and used properly, presentation aids will help you get your message across clearly and convincingly. Whatever support you are using should be prepared ready to use during your rehearsal, which is the subject of the next chapter.

KEY POINTS

❏ Only use support aids when it is the best way to get a point across.
❏ Select aids appropriate to the information you want to convey and the impact you want to create.
❏ Use your imagination for the best results.
❏ Make your aids clear and easy to understand.
❏ Do not let them come between you and the audience.

5

REHEARSING

Some people do not bother rehearsing. Perhaps they feel that, having prepared their talk carefully, they know what they want to say well enough to deliver it without further work. Others simply read silently through their notes to become familiar with the ideas they want to convey. Neither approach is sufficient, even for experienced presenters who know their subject intimately.

At least one full rehearsal, including any support aids, is essential before a presentation of any importance. A proper rehearsal is as close as possible to the real thing. Hearing yourself speak the words aloud makes you familiar with your message as you have planned to present it (this is much harder to do by silent reading). If you do not rehearse properly it is easy to deviate from your carefully prepared message and risk losing much of its impact. You may elaborate some points, give less time to others, introduce new ideas that spring to mind or change the examples you use to illustrate points.

You can over-rehearse, however, and become too familiar with what you want to say. One result is that your ideas will not feel as fresh and significant as before and you will find it difficult to deliver them spontaneously with enthusiasm. The audience will sense the lack of enthusiasm and it will have a negative impact. You can also become overconfident that you know what you want to say. As a result you may tempted to ignore your notes or script occasionally and then inadvertently deviate from your message.

Rehearsal is an opportunity to experience, as closely as possible, what it will be like on the day. This may include answering questions, which you should rehearse if this is a possibility. It is also your last opportunity to check and, if necessary, fine-tune your message.

This chapter will help you to:

❑ rehearse delivering your message;
❑ involve and respond to your audience;
❑ practise responding to audience questions;
❑ assess and fine-tune your presentation;
❑ prepare your final presentation notes or script.

One of the major benefits of rehearsal is that it gives you the confidence of knowing you can remember what you want to say. On the day, however nervous you feel, once you start speaking you will find that what you want to say comes to you automatically with just a little prompting from your notes or script.

WHEN AND HOW TO REHEARSE

Never leave your rehearsal until the last minute. You should leave sufficient time afterwards to make any necessary changes to your talk or support aids. Significant changes may necessitate another full rehearsal to become familiar with the changes. The more fine-tuning you think could be required the more time you should allow between rehearsal and the presentation. Group presentations, for example, where you are delivering one part of a collective message, will require more time. You need to ensure that all the elements are linked effectively and well integrated to convey a single, cohesive message.

Rehearsal needs to be planned and conducted properly. You should not simply squeeze it into the occasional spare five minutes. At least one full rehearsal is necessary, which will last the duration of your presentation and often longer (many people initially overestimate how much information they can convey in a specified time). The purpose is to:

❑ learn the structure and content of the message you want to convey (but not the words);
❑ practise expressing your ideas using the examples and other devices you have chosen;
❑ check that you are conveying your message effectively.

If you are anxious about giving a presentation, as most people are, it is tempting to learn what you want to say word for word. This can make life difficult for you. First, it puts more pressure on you to remember exactly what you wanted to say. Second, delivering a memorised speech effectively (so that you sound animated and natural) requires considerable skill which only comes with special training.

A presentation should sound spontaneous. The best way to achieve this, whether you intend talking from memory, notes or a script, is to make yourself fully familiar with your message and the points you want to make. You rehearse just enough to achieve this but without memorising the words to express your ideas. These will come to you automatically during your presentation, just as in everyday conversation, so that you are naturally spontaneous.

Even speakers who read a prepared speech from an autocue often change the wording, saying what springs to mind rather than what is written, so that they sound spontaneous. It is possible, though highly unlikely, that you could be required to deliver a speech word for word as it is written (eg for legal reasons or if your comments will be a matter of record). If this happens it suggests that the presentation is of particular importance and you should consider seeking professional help if you want to make your delivery sound spontaneous.

An important benefit of retaining spontaneity is that you can respond more intuitively to the audience, as you would in a normal conversation. If you sense that some people are not listening, for example, or do not fully grasp what you are saying, you may stress a point more forcefully or repeat something in a different way. This type of flexible response, reacting to your audience, is impossible if you are sticking hard and fast to a prepared text.

How much you should rehearse depends on how quickly you memorise your message. You want to be able to recall the points you want to make, and the examples you have chosen, but not the words to express them. If you intend using notes or a script as a prompt obviously you will require less rehearsal than if you want to deliver your presentation completely from memory.

Getting feedback

As well as helping you to become familiar with your message rehearsal gives you a chance to assess the effectiveness of your message and your delivery. To do this you need feedback. One source of feedback is a professional adviser on presentation. There are many companies offering specialist training and advice on delivering presentations. They provide help in preparing for specific events as well as general presentation skills training.

Many of these training companies use closed-circuit television to record clients' mock presentations or rehearsals. The training consultant uses the video recording to highlight the client's strengths and weaknesses and offer guidance on improving both the message and the delivery technique. Seeing and hearing yourself delivering a presentation is an excellent way to learn provided it is accompanied by expert feedback and coaching. With the current widespread use of camcorders it would be relatively easy to arrange to record your rehearsal to gain an impression of your performance. Without expert feedback, however, you will not gain the full benefit.

You can use either video or audio recording to get an impression of how you will come across to your audience. You will not have expert guidance on how you could improve your delivery but there are tips later in this chapter on aspects of your performance you could analyse.

The next best thing to professional feedback is to rehearse in front of an audience and ask them to comment. The ideal people would be those you can trust to give you an honest assessment. Their comments on your message and the way it is structured and explained can be particularly useful. You will also get a sense of what it is like to deliver your talk in front of an audience and answer their questions. There are some tips later in this chapter on how you can help your rehearsal audience to give you constructive feedback.

If you are going to rehearse in front of an audience it is a good idea to have a full rehearsal by yourself beforehand. The reason is that many people overestimate the amount of information which can be conveyed in a specified time. If you need to make major cuts you should try to do this before you rehearse with an audience.

Methods of rehearsal

Some people like to read silently through their presentation. Although this can help you to memorise the points you want to make it is not as effective as speaking your words aloud. This is a better aid to memory, because it mimics the real thing, and you will know what it is like hearing yourself speak to an audience. Running through the complete presentation is better than doing it piecemeal. You should make time for at least one continuous run through, using your presentation aids, even if you start by rehearsing piecemeal.

Computer software is available designed specifically to help with rehearsal (and delivery) of presentations. *Harvard Spotlight for Windows* works with any Windows-based presentation graphics package. The screen shows the current slide (as the audience sees it if you are using it to deliver your presentation) and provides on-screen chalk and pointer tools to highlight information on the slide. The corresponding presentation notes are displayed at the same time on the speaker's screen. Timing and pacing indicators display the times allocated to each slide as well as elapsed time. If you fall behind or move ahead of the planned timing, indicators warn you to speed up or slow down. Even if you are not using the software to deliver your presentation the timing indicators can be useful in rehearsal. The drawback, however, is that you come to rely on the prompts. You will miss them if you do not have them on the day. In rehearsal you need to mimic the real thing as closely as possible.

If you intend presenting from memory or notes the outline you prepared when planning your talk (see page 45) is a good starting-point for your rehearsal. It contains all your key points, links and illustrative examples which you have checked against audience needs (including their level of understanding). If you have prepared a full script for your delivery you can use this for rehearsal.

Rehearsal should help you learn to deliver your prepared speech in as natural a way as possible. You want to be able to speak confidently and spontaneously while making regular eye contact across the whole audience. You should never speak while looking away from the audience. In rehearsal, therefore, you should look down at your notes or script, scan what you want to say next, look up at the audience and then say it. The drill suggested by Lee Bowman (see Exercise) is valuable because it helps to overcome the common tendency of people to race through a presentation without giving people time to digest what they are saying.

People generally have a tendency to talk too quickly in presentations. Some people talk fast naturally and this is no problem provided others can fully understand them. What does cause a problem, however, is not pausing appropriately between discrete points and ideas.

Nervousness alters our sense of time so we perceive the slightest hesitancy as an eternity. The more nervous we are the more distorted our sense of time. We sense pauses as embarrassing, elongated silences whereas to the audience we are just pausing for thought. Ask someone to read a short piece of text to you without pausing and you will recognise the importance of pausing in conveying meaning.

Normal conversation is punctuated by silences. We pause while we gauge the reaction to what we have just said and to think of what we want to say next. This gives speech its natural rhythm and pace, helping to give emphasis and meaning to what we say. It also helps people to understand what we are saying because it gives them time to digest each thought and

EXERCISE

Lee Bowman, in his book *High Impact Business Presentations* with Andrew Croft, suggests a very good drill which can be used in rehearsal. Bowman heads an international consultancy on spoken communication. Their approach is to enable people to use their normal, relaxed style of conversation in formal presentations. The technique is designed to get you into the habit of pausing between thoughts, as you do in normal conversation. In essence the drill is to:

❑ Glance down at your outline or script and take in as many words as possible (in practice you can only remember several at most).
❑ Look up, establish eye contact with your audience and pause briefly.
❑ Speak the words and then pause while maintaining eye contact.
❑ Look down again and take in the next words.

This cycle is repeated until the end of your talk. Bowman says that although it is unnatural to break sentences or thoughts in this way it gets you accustomed to pausing. (Failing to pause long enough between ideas is one of the most common failings in making presentations.) This is essential to allow your audience time to absorb what you have said. It also gives the impression that you are thinking about what you are going to say, as you do in normal conversation. As you become more familiar with your message you can grasp whole ideas with each glance and your delivery becomes less and less stilted but you retain the all-important pauses.

place it in context before hearing the next thought. Lee Bowman's drill is designed to force you to pause and, with practice, learn how to pause naturally between thoughts.

INVOLVING AND RESPONDING TO YOUR AUDIENCE

When you rehearse in front of an audience you have the opportunity to practise involving them, reading their reaction to what you say and responding appropriately. In normal conversation we are continually gauging the reaction of the people we are addressing. We look at their eyes, their facial expression and their general demeanour to sense whether they are listening and understand what we have just said. Although we may be doing all the talking, the communication is two-way. If we sense that some people are not listening, for example, we might raise our voice, change our tone or ask a question to gain their attention. Much of this happens automatically and we are unaware of it. It is second nature.

You want to achieve a similar pattern of two-way communication with your audience in a presentation. You need to know how they are reacting to what you say so you can make them listen when they are not listening, help them understand when they are confused, and so on.

With large audiences obviously you cannot 'read' and respond to every individual at once. However, you can aim to keep everyone listening and following your message by varying your voice, using silence, gestures and repetition when you sense that it is needed. This might sound difficult but, if you have mastered the knack of speaking spontaneously, your response to the audience will come naturally. Once you have learnt your message during rehearsal you will find it much easier to be attentive to audience reaction because you will not have to concentrate so much on what you want to say.

Eye contact plays an important role in everyday conversation. When you look at people you gain their attention, so they are primed to listen to what you say. In normal situations we establish eye contact, look away and then re-establish contact spontaneously throughout a conversation.

In the unusual setting of a presentation we can easily lose this natural component of communication. If we are galvanised by nerves we tend to fix our gaze, perhaps on our notes or some point in the room. This can create a negative impression. Try to recall situations where people have been talking to you but have avoided looking you in the eyes. They can come across as being untruthful or unsure of what they are saying. Maintaining eye contact constantly can be equally negative. It feels unnatural and can come across as oppressive and even intimidating.

The two key times for eye contact are just before we start making a point and when we conclude the point. First we are establishing contact, indicating that we have something significant to say and making sure we have their attention. Making eye contact as we conclude the point says we are looking for an indication of whether we have been heard and understood. If we look away at this stage it suggests to the audience that the point we have made is not that significant. It is important not to speak while glancing at your notes. Always look up and re-establish eye contact with the audience first.

Eye contact and pauses work in tandem. The importance of pausing between ideas to give people time to digest what we have said has already been stressed (page 72). Pauses can also be used to gain attention and heighten expectation. When we want to tell someone something significant we normally make a signal, such as calling their name or making a preliminary remark, and then wait to make eye contact before we deliver our message. Similarly, if we are talking and we sense our audience is momentarily distracted we pause, indicating that we are waiting for their attention again before we continue.

Periods of silence, or extended pauses, can be very useful to regain audience attention. Silence in the midst of sound can be as effective as sound in the midst of silence in getting someone's attention. To avoid alienating those who are already attentive, and probably looking at you, you can refer to your notes or script while you pause, as if you are thinking carefully about your next comment.

Throughout your presentation you need to watch and analyse audience reactions and behaviour so that you can respond appropriately. Some examples of what to look for and what it may signify are listed in Table 5.1. If you are rehearsing in front of an audience you can make a mental note of how individuals react and ask them afterwards whether your analysis of their behaviour is accurate.

You will generally know intuitively how you need to respond to various signs from the audience. If some people look

Table 5.1 *Audience behaviour and its possible meaning*

Audience reaction	Possible meaning
Looking away while you are speaking	Distracted or disinterested
Shaking the head	Disagreement or disapproval
A quizzical look	Confused, does not understand, bored or tired
A nod	Agreement or approval
Shuffling about	Bored, irritated or uncomfortable

confused, for example, perhaps you need to slow down or explain that particular point again in a different way. If they are distracted you could use silence or pose a rhetorical question. If they seem bored you could quicken the pace of your talk or introduce a visual aid. If there is a sudden visible change in their attitude, could it be something you have just said? If they appear to disagree perhaps you need to give further supporting evidence of the point you have just made. If they agree you might benefit from consolidating what you have said with another example.

As soon as you stand to speak you need to create a dialogue: you speak, the audience reacts, you speak in response to the reaction. If you are achieving a conversational style your audience will feel you are talking with them and not at them. They will feel involved. Remember too that mood is infectious. If you do not show enthusiasm for your message neither will your audience.

RESPONDING TO QUESTIONS

If there is a possibility of you being asked questions, particularly in front of the whole audience rather than later in relative privacy, you should rehearse answering questions. Treat them as an integral part of your presentation because the way you respond can create a strong impression among the audience. Questions and answers are like bubble quotes in cartoons – they stand out. Also remember that people form impressions based on what they can observe rather than reality. A single unreasoned comment, perhaps made quickly in response to a question which took you by surprise, could give them an unjustly negative impression of you.

When you do not have an audience for your rehearsal you have to rely purely on formulating your own questions. Although this might seem artificial you are in the best position to know what questions are most likely to be asked. You should have considered this, and what you could say in response, during your preparation (see page 49). Simply select a sample of these questions at random during your rehearsal and answer them aloud.

If you have an audience you can ask them to select questions from those you have identified. Answer a few of these and then ask them for their own questions and some of your questions modified. This will help you become more accustomed to answering spontaneously without preparation. You must be prepared for the unexpected.

In most situations you will want to avoid inviting questions during your main talk, unless you want to check that the audience understand what you have said or want other feedback. If someone interrupts you with a question you have a choice. If your answer will strengthen the point you have just made, and you can answer it briefly, you might decide to answer it there and then. However, if answering it means interrupting the flow of your message it is best to say that you will note the question and answer it at the appropriate time. If you choose this course, do make a note of it and then be sure to answer it before any others.

In some situations, such as open meetings and business pitches, you may need to treat questions and your answers as an integral part of the ongoing presentation, answering each question as it arises. If a question highlights a possible flaw or gap in your argument and you say you will answer it later your audience may feel you are evading the issue. This can distract them from listening to the rest of your message.

Questions are not always simply an appeal for information. They can be asked to satisfy various needs, some of which you may have identified when analysing your audience. For example, people asking questions might be seeking to:

❑ gain attention or approval;
❑ display their expertise;
❑ air their own concerns;
❑ lead you on to another subject, or away from one;
❑ disrupt your speech or discredit your opinion.

You need to think quickly on your feet and ask yourself, 'Why is this person asking this particular question?'

Inflammatory and loaded questions are more common at certain types of event, such as Annual General Meetings and sometimes inter-departmental meetings. When a question is clearly intended to goad you into a rash response or an argument it is often best to make a benign comment. For example, you could say, 'Do you really think that's true? It sounds more like a loaded question to me', and then pass on to the next question. Alternatively it may be appropriate to ask, 'What exactly is your question?' Whenever a difficult situation like this arises you should aim to generate a sympathetic response among the rest of your audience. Never let your response sound belittling of the questioner. Some possible responses to different types of question are shown in Table 5.2.

Here are some general guidelines for answering audience questions.

❑ Listen carefully, keeping an open mind until you have heard the full question. If it is several questions in one, make a note of each part.
❑ If the question is not clear ask for clarification or paraphrase what you think the question is. Repeat the question, if necessary, so that everyone has heard it.
❑ Pause for thought before answering, even if you already know what you want to say. It is a compliment to the

Table 5.2 *Ways of answering different types of question*

Type of question	Possible response
Several questions in one	Ask what the main question is and answer that
One which makes an incorrect presumption	Tactfully point out the mistake and then answer the question if it is still relevant
Hostile	Express understanding of the comment, if reasonable, but explain why you have said what they are reacting against
Rambling	Wait a reasonable time and then interrupt and ask what the question is
Asking you to make an inappropriate commitment	State clearly that you cannot make the commitment and then, if appropriate, explain briefly why not
Hypothetical	If an answer is appropriate state clearly that your answer refers to the hypothetical situation

questioner, who has asked a thought-provoking question, shows the audience you are going to give a thoughtful response and stops you making unguarded comments.

❏ Try to decide from the questioner's manner and tone of voice if there is a hidden reason for the question.

❏ If you do not have an answer, say so. No one is expected to have all the answers. If you can research an answer you can offer to come back to the questioner later (never try to bluff an answer). Alternatively you can ask if anyone in the audience can answer the question.

❏ If it is a complex question divide it into parts and state which part you are answering as you give your response.

❑ Focus on what you want to say, quickly decide your main points and any supporting example.

❑ Try to relate your answers to points you have made in your talk. Avoid raising new points.

❑ If your answer must be more than a few sentences give it structure – an introduction, middle and conclusion.

❑ Make eye contact with the questioner and start to speak. Then, if it is a lengthy answer, address the whole audience and return to the questioner before you finish.

❑ Answer as briefly and simply as possible. This reflects clear thinking. If the questioner has hit on a pet subject of yours do not be tempted to elaborate.

❑ If the question highlights a weakness in your argument avoid becoming defensive and trying to justify yourself. If applicable, say you are aware of this and have been giving it thought.

Answering questions can be the most challenging part of a presentation. The best advice is to be yourself. If you appear honest and fair in your responses the audience generally will not even notice if you do not give full answers to all the questions.

ASSESSING AND FINE-TUNING YOUR PRESENTATION

To fine-tune the content and delivery of your presentation first you need feedback. Sources of feedback were examined earlier. The more structured the feedback the more useful it is. The following sections give some tips on what sort of feedback you need.

Your message

This is your last opportunity to make considered changes in the content and timing of your presentation. The series of questions below may help you to gather structured feedback. If you are lucky enough to have an audience for your rehearsal you can give these questions to them beforehand and ask them to read them so they know what to watch for during your presentation.

If you collate their responses afterwards it will help you to decide what changes, if any, you need to make.

❏ Did my introduction:
  - grab your attention?

✎

_____

_____

_____

  - make you want to hear more?

✎

_____

_____

_____

❏ Did I explain my ideas well?

✎

_____

_____

_____

❏ Did the sequence of ideas seem logical?

✎

_____

_____

_____

❏ Was my talk easy to follow?

✎

_____

_____

_____

❏ Was anything I said irrelevant or superfluous?

❏ Did I cover all the relevant points?

❏ Were my examples, anecdotes, etc:
  – relevant?

  – good illustrations of the points I was making?

❏ In communicating my ideas, were the slides and other aids
  I used:
  – necessary?

– relevant?

✎

_____

_____

_____

– clear?

✎

_____

_____

_____

– effective?

✎

_____

_____

_____

❏ Did I labour any points unnecessarily?

✎

_____

_____

_____

❏ Did I skip over any points?

✎

_____

_____

_____

❏ Was any information missing?

✎
_____

_____

_____

❏ Did I pitch the language at the right level?

✎
_____

_____

_____

❏ Was there a clear central theme?

✎
_____

_____

_____

❏ Did my conclusion:
  – tie all my ideas together?

  ✎
  _____

  _____

  _____

  – leave you with a buzz?

  ✎
  _____

  _____

  _____

❑ What was my overriding message?

✎

_____

_____

_____

❑ Did the talk seem too short or overlong for the subject?

✎

_____

_____

_____

❑ Did I come across as knowing what I was talking about?

✎

_____

_____

_____

❑ Did you find the talk interesting?

✎

_____

_____

_____

❑ Did your interest flag at any stage?

✎

_____

_____

_____

❑ What did you gain by listening to my talk?

❑ Did it meet your expectations?

❑ How much of what I said can you recall?

❑ Who would benefit most from listening to my talk?

❑ What was your overall feeling when I finished?

You can add or delete questions depending on the type of presentation you are making. The purpose of the questions is self-evident. The structured feedback you get can indicate whether you achieved your objectives, you need to rearrange ideas, give more explanation of some points and less of others, delete material, and so on.

If you make major changes, particularly in the sequence of ideas, you will need further rehearsal to become accustomed to them. The most realistic rehearsal is in front of an audience. If you cut or rearrange material, therefore, it is best to do this before involving your audience so that they experience the nearest thing to the finished talk.

There should a balance in the time you spend explaining various points, giving points of equal importance a similar amount of time. Feedback from an audience will help you to assess whether you have laboured or skipped over any specific points. If you have used good examples and other devices to explain your ideas it is surprising how little time you need to convey them effectively. If you have a choice of how long you speak it is often better to err on the short side and leave extra time for questions and answers. After about 18–20 minutes it becomes much harder to sustain people's attention. Even so, many presentations, at conferences for example, are routinely allotted twice this amount of time.

During rehearsals keep a check on the time you spend on each discrete part of your presentation. The more accustomed you are to judging your timing the easier it will be to keep on track on the day.

Your delivery

Improving the way you deliver your presentation is not as easy as fine-tuning your message. However, the following questions will help to make you aware of what your audience may sense. Again, if you are rehearsing with an audience their answers to these questions will provide valuable feedback.

❑ Did my personality come across, ie did you recognise me in the way I delivered my talk?

❑ Did I always speak:
– clearly?

– confidently?

– in a relaxed way?

❑ At any time did you fail to understand what I was saying?

❏ Did I stumble over any particular sentences?

_____

_____

_____

❏ Did my voice have rhythm and help to convey meaning?

_____

_____

_____

❏ Did I sound and appear enthusiastic about the subject?

_____

_____

_____

❏ Did I sound uncertain about what I was saying at any time?

_____

_____

_____

❏ Did I sound unconvincing at any time?

_____

_____

_____

❏ Did you notice if I had any distracting mannerisms?

✎

_____

_____

_____

❏ When I used my presentation aids:
 – did they ever interrupt the flow of ideas?

✎

_____

_____

_____

 – did I ever distract you from the aid?

✎

_____

_____

_____

 – did you notice any hiccups in the way I used them?

✎

_____

_____

_____

❏ Did you feel that I was interested in your reaction to what I was saying?

✎

_____

_____

_____

❑ Did I appear to be ignoring you at any time?

_____

_____

_____

❑ When I answered your questions:
   – did I answer the questions you had asked?

_____

_____

_____

   – were my answers what you were seeking?

_____

_____

_____

   – did I convey them effectively?

_____

_____

_____

   – did I sound confident in my responses?

_____

_____

_____

Many people in prominent positions, particularly those holding public office and top executive posts, take advantage of professional coaching to improve their presentation delivery technique. Often this is to prepare for media interviews which present particular problems because of things such as editing, time constraints and interrogation by skilled reporters.

Sometimes coaching is designed to mould a new public persona, teaching individuals how to alter their voice and body language to portray very specific characteristics. Margaret Thatcher is probably the most well-known example and the record shows that the results are not always positive.

Every person can benefit from professional presentation training. However, only a small proportion of training seeks to change people. Mostly it helps them to overcome the unnatural nature of the situation so that they can behave more like their usual selves. That is the best advice you can follow. Be yourself.

The following three sections contain comments about voice, body language and grooming. These are mostly observations about how an audience may perceive different characteristics. They are not meant to provide firm guidance on what you should aim to achieve. You may want to heed some points if you feel that they will create a more positive impression among your audience, but beware trying to be something you are not. It is very difficult to let your personality shine through if you continually have to think about how you are behaving and speaking.

Voice

The voice brings words to life spontaneously when we speak. It is a part of our natural talent for communication. Only a tiny proportion of people habitually speak with no colour in their voice.

The aspects of speech which help to give it rhythm and convey meaning include:

Pitch. Variation in pitch helps to give colour to the voice. Heightened pitch with little variation suggests nervousness.

Heightened pitch with variation is more indicative of excitement or enthusiasm. An unvarying low pitch makes us sound disinterested, tired or depressed.

Volume. Volume gives emphasis. Depending on the circumstances, both raising and lowering the volume of your voice can highlight a particular point or phrase. A sudden, significant fall or rise in volume can also get people's attention.

Speed. You can make a point more emphatically by slowing the speed at which you speak. A progressive increase in speed throughout a sentence or two creates a sense of urgency or excitement.

Pauses. The importance of pauses was stressed earlier (page 72). Silence between words, phrases and sentences contributes to the rhythm of speech and helps to convey meaning. It can also grab attention and heighten expectation.

In everyday conversation each of these components is orchestrated automatically. In a presentation, however, nervousness can make it difficult for us to speak with our normal fluency and rhythm. If you have rehearsed with an audience their feedback may have highlighted negative effects on your voice due to nervousness. The most common effect is disruption of our natural rhythm of speech. One of the benefits of rehearsal is that we can learn where we want to pause for effect, increase our pace or speak with greater emphasis. If, in the stress of the situation, you find it difficult to retain your normal conversational style you can add this information to your notes or script to help you with your delivery.

People with strong accents sometimes panic at the thought of speaking in public. They think the audience may find it difficult to understand them and even be irritated by the accent. However broad an accent, if it can be understood in everyday conversation it will be understood in a presentation. (If you have a strong accent you will know from experience if people have difficulty understanding any particular words or phrases.) Having an accent can even be a bonus. It can provide a refreshing change for an audience, particularly towards the end of a day-long conference. Some accents have a particular rhythm which make them intrinsically pleasing to hear.

Body language

Posture, gestures, facial expression and eye contact convey a lot of information. Most of this is perceived unconsciously but it is nonetheless powerful, influencing how both speaker and message are perceived. Natural eye contact (see page 74), gestures and facial expressions in particular can be distorted in the stressful situation of a presentation.

Like the texture of speech, body language is a natural response. The more self-confidence you can build through rehearsal, and the more conversational the style of speaking you achieve, the more natural your body language will be. Concentrate on getting your message across effectively and your body language should not be a problem.

Many experienced presenters appear less animated on stage than in more informal settings. Sometimes this is because they deliberately restrict their movement during a presentation. If you watch speakers at conferences you will notice that some hold the sides of the lectern and perhaps just occasionally lift a hand to gesture. This is one method that can be used to prevent unnecessary gesturing or fidgeting caused by nervousness which, if excessive, can distract the audience from what the presenter is saying.

Some people worry about showing visible signs of nervousness, such as shaking hands. Unless you are within feet of the audience no one will notice. Even then it will not be as noticeable as it feels. The main focus for any audience, most of the time, is the presenter's face. For this reason you may find that you need to force yourself to smile when you take the stage and until you get into the swing of the presentation and your natural enthusiasm takes over.

Grooming

Personal style is a reflection of our personality. We live it and need to feel comfortable with it. Within these confines, however, most of us adapt according to the occasion. Conventions about what is suitable dress for different situations have relaxed considerably but your appearance is still important. It can reflect your attitude towards the audience, your work and your organisation. It can also be a reflection of the style and efficiency of your organisation or department. First impressions stick and, whether it is just or not, people often form their strongest opinion of us based on our appearance.

The image you want to create is one of caring about your appearance. A careless appearance can rub off on your opinions. Beyond that all you need to worry about is not providing the audience (or you) with a distraction from your talk.

It is important to dress in a way that makes you feel comfortable and confident. For important occasions it is advisable to decide well beforehand what you will wear. Putting on a few extra pounds can make you feel uncomfortable and less confident if the clothes are ill-fitting. Also consider the likely temperature at the venue and choose clothes that will remain comfortable despite feeling hot and bothered in the stress of the moment.

PREPARING DELIVERY NOTES

Rehearsal is the time to prepare the final version of your notes or script, if you are using them, complete with any annotations to support your delivery.

To recap, the advantages of delivering from notes are that:

❑ Choosing words spontaneously to explain your ideas sounds more natural and convincing.
❑ It is easier to remain flexible to respond to your audience.
❑ It helps you become more involved with your message.

Some people prefer to have the support of a full script, but even this can be annotated or highlighted to help retain spontaneity.

When you are satisfied that you have got your message right and are familiar with how you want to present it, you can prepare your delivery notes or annotated script. To prepare notes you need to condense your outline so that it will fit on small, unobtrusive cards which you can number in sequence and use as an *aide-mémoire* during your presentation. Notes typically contain:

❑ Key words or phrases to help you recall each step of your message and the relevant descriptive devices.
❑ Cues for when to use aids.
❑ The full text of any information you want to speak or write word for word.

Some people like to use concise sentences but the fewer the words the better. Graphics can be used, or flow charts to show a sequence of ideas. Use whatever works best for you but make it easy to read at a glance. Use a large typeface and plenty of space.

A particular danger with notes is that you can quite easily wander unintentionally and elaborate points. If you are using them you must discipline yourself to follow them rigorously.

Annotating a script or highlighting words or phrases can help you to give proper emphasis and make your talk sound more spontaneous. Make a note during your rehearsals of how you want to vary your delivery at particular points. Then indicate this on your script so that you can recognise it at a glance.

Around the same time as your rehearsal it is advisable to check that nothing relating to your presentation requires action. If you intend sending handouts to audience members before the event, for example, will these be available on time? And do you know where to send them? Other things you may need to check include your travel arrangements and accommodation. If you are organising the event there are many things to check (seating, lighting, equipment, catering, confirmation of attendance, etc) but this is another subject on which there are many books.

Rehearsing adequately will increase your confidence. When you take the stage on the day, even if you are trembling with fear, you will know that you have already delivered the same presentation successfully in rehearsal. Once you have started, all your preparation will kick into action and support you through to a successful conclusion.

KEY POINTS

❑ Rehearse to become familiar with your storyline and not the words of your story – choose those as you speak so that your delivery is truly spontaneous.

❑ Practise making regular eye contact with the audience, observing them and reading and responding to their reactions.

❑ Use your rehearsal to fine-tune your message and your delivery technique.

❑ Use the experience of your rehearsal to prepare notes or script annotations to use as an *aide-mémoire* on the day.

ON THE DAY

Even after carefully planning and rehearsing a presentation many people are worried by the thought that something will go wrong on the day. Fear is your worst enemy – fear of forgetting what you intended to say, of making a fool of yourself, and fear that the audience will not respond in the way that you want.

Confidence in being able to spark enthusiasm in your audience and keep them interested is the key to successful delivery. If you have prepared adequately you really should not have any problem delivering an effective presentation. This chapter contains some last-minute tips designed to help bolster your confidence.

PREVENTING LAST-MINUTE HITCHES

Executive air-travellers have been known to lose their luggage *en route* to important meetings and arrive minus clean shirt, well-pressed suit and, most disastrously, their presentation notes and slides. Even if you are speaking in the office next door last minute hitches can ruin a well-prepared presentation.

Most things which could cause a last-minute upset can be avoided or quickly put right if you make final checks. For example:

Before you set out
❑ Plan to leave with enough time to arrive early even if delayed *en route*.

❏ Think about whether there have been any last-minute developments which affect the content of your talk, eg national news, in-house policy decisions. Do you need to amend your talk or prepare any additional comments?

❏ Check that you have your notes, perhaps even a duplicate set, and they are in the right order.

❏ Check your visual aids if they are not already at the venue. Do you have the markers or pens you need for the flip chart or overhead projector?

❏ Ensure you have everything you need for personal comfort, eg glasses, pills for hay fever, handkerchief for a running nose.

❏ Look in the mirror to check that you look presentable and are happy with your appearance.

When you arrive

❏ Check that the time of your presentation has not been changed.

❏ Check your visual aids if they were sent earlier to the venue.

❏ If you are using any equipment check that it is in position and working. Are spares readily available, eg a replacement bulb for the slide projector?

❏ Does the seating arrangement give your audience good visibility? For small gatherings, does it focus audience attention towards where you will stand?

❏ Does the lighting and temperature provide a comfortable environment?

❏ Is there anything which might distract the audience, eg charts from previous speakers, unused equipment?

Even if some of these things are not your responsibility you may like to check them if only to put your mind at rest. Eliminating potential hitches will prevent you worrying unnecessarily.

USING STAGE FRIGHT TO ADVANTAGE

Even the most experienced and self-confident presenters get nervous before an important presentation. Stage fright can be a major problem. It makes you feel bad and can get in the way of giving your best performance. But it can also work for you. Professional actors worry if they do not feel nervous before a performance. They know that the symptoms of stage fright – butterflies, sweaty palms, trembling – reflect the high level of nervous energy they need to give a good performance. That same energy can help you give a lively, attention-grabbing presentation.

CASE STUDY

The chairmen of two leading British companies suffered a similar problem. Despite their professional success they lacked confidence in speaking to large audiences. In fact, they were terrified every time they had to make a formal presentation. One always fainted shortly after taking the stage, the other stumbled over his words almost incoherently. After training both men became competent speakers, having learnt to control their fear of the situation. They learnt that nervousness was natural and could be channelled into a lively, animated performance.

The physical signs of excitement and stage fright are much the same. In both cases there is a high level of adrenalin in the blood, which is a biological response priming the body to exert extra energy. Until that energy is used purposively, eg leaping up and down and screaming with delight when we are excited, it manifests in other ways. Think of the symptoms of stage fright as a sign that your body is charged with energy and try to channel it into delivering your message. You will probably still feel weak at the knees and jittery but what the audience will see is a dynamic presenter. If you feel you need a focus for excess nervous energy try tensing your muscles, such as curling your toes in your shoes.

When you have approached a presentation sensibly there is no rational reason why you should fear being unable to deliver it successfully. If you have prepared carefully you should be confident about your message and believe in what you are saying. You will have demonstrated to yourself that you can do it when you rehearsed. Looking your best will also help you believe in yourself and increase your self-confidence.

One of the greatest fears presenters have is of 'drying up' or losing their train of thought. This is not a major problem even if it happens. You can minimise the risk by using your finger as a marker on your notes or script. If it does happen, however, just follow these steps:

❑ Calmly look down at your notes and find your place.
❑ Pause to collect your thoughts (remember pauses are natural).
❑ Look up and re-establish eye contact with the audience.
❑ Continue speaking where you left off, repeating your last few words if you need to re-establish continuity.

None of these comments are going to stop you feeling nervous (being too relaxed would rob you of vitality anyway). However, they should help you to put your feelings in perspective, recognising them for what they are – your body telling you that you are ready for action.

YOUR DELIVERY CHECKLIST

The following sections summarise key points on delivering your presentation effectively. You can use them as a reminder of what you aimed to achieve during your rehearsal.

Involving and responding to your audience
❑ Start to establish a rapport with your audience as soon as possible – when you stand to speak make eye contact and scan the entire audience.
❑ Capture their interest with your introduction – imbue it with energy and enthusiasm.
❑ Maintain regular eye contact with all parts of your audience – the two most important times are just before you start making a point and just before you conclude a point.

❑ 'Read' your audience continually, trying to sense whether you have their attention and how they are reacting to what you say.

❑ Respond appropriately to their feelings (lack of interest, confusion, disagreement, etc) through your words and voice.

❑ Try to maintain spontaneity throughout your talk.

❑ Conclude emphatically, inspiring your audience.

Using your notes or script

❑ Look down and scan the point you want to make.

❑ Look up, re-establish eye contact and pause briefly.

❑ Make your point and then pause while maintaining eye contact.

❑ Look down and take in your next point – then keep repeating the exercise.

❑ If you are using an autocue, establish a routine of looking away from the screen so that you do not appear to be continually staring at the audience.

Presentation aids

❑ Do not let your aids compete with you for audience attention.

❑ Introduce your aid and then remain silent while the audience takes in the information.

❑ When the audience is viewing an aid only talk if it is absolutely necessary.

❑ If you are writing or drawing do not labour over it but make sure it is clear and large enough for all to see.

❑ Once an aid has served its purpose remove it or hide it from view.

❑ Re-establish eye contact before you resume talking.

Answering questions

❑ Make sure you and the whole audience understand the question asked.

❑ Pause for thought before answering (if you do not have an answer, say so).

❑ Answer complex or multiple questions in discrete parts.

❑ Keep your answers as short and simple as possible.

❏ Do not become defensive if a questioner highlights a gap or flaw in your argument.
❏ Treat your answers as part of your talk, observing your audience to ensure they understand.

Experience is the best way to become better at giving presentations but do not expect it to become any easier or less scary. The majority of people are, and always will be, nervous before giving a presentation. What experience teaches you, however, is that the expectation is worse than the reality. When you have done it once you will have more confidence in being able to rely on your preparation to help you deliver an effective presentation.

KEY POINTS

❏ Before your presentation make checks to prevent avoidable hitches.
❏ Use your nervous energy to project a dynamic image and bring your subject alive – mood is infectious.
❏ Observe your audience and respond to the shifting tides of their attention, interest and understanding.
❏ Give an animated performance and you will leave them with a lasting impression.

POSTSCRIPT - TRAINING COURSES

Many people find that receiving professional training in presentation skills gives them extra confidence. Rehearsing with an expert coach and getting immediate feedback with tips on how to improve your delivery technique can create a real sense of empowerment. Being on a course with others who are in a similar situation also provides a stimulating learning environment and an opportunity to share experiences and concerns.

Presentation skills training is widely available. Courses are offered by business schools, professional bodies, management training centres, general training organisations and specialist consultants. Many businesses provide their managers with training in-house using their own trainers or external consultants.

Most courses are of one, two or three days duration. Some are residential. Also available are seminars, individual coaching, computer-based training and videos with course materials. Some specialist companies offer training in the use of presentation graphics software packages.

Presentation skills courses vary in their structure and approach but closed-circuit television is used commonly to record delegates making short presentations. This recorded performance is used as a basis for the trainer and other delegates to give feedback. Various practical exercises are used to build skills and help individuals improve their ability to deliver effective presentations.

The number of delegates on courses varies. Often numbers are restricted, say to six, so that each delegate receives adequate personal attention. Larger groups are sometimes split into small syndicates for role plays and other practical exercises.

Some courses are deliberately designed for all levels of management so that delegates will experience presenting to people of varying levels of seniority, as happens often in real life situations.

The scope of courses varies. There are foundation as well as advanced courses. Areas covered may include:

❑ awareness of audience needs and expectations;
❑ structuring a presentation so that it is clear and logical;
❑ choosing the words to make your ideas clear and striking;
❑ choosing, designing and using appropriate visual aids;
❑ effective delivery technique;
❑ dealing with questions effectively;
❑ channelling and coping with nervousness;
❑ preparing the venue.

Topics such as body language, image and voice projection may be included but most courses aim to build confidence and instil a positive attitude rather than change delegates' basic behaviour.

Courses may be tailored to varying degrees. Individual coaching can be tailored very specifically to the needs of the individual, perhaps to hone particular skills or in preparation for a specific presentation. A course designed for a specific company may include reference to its products and services, markets and any particular house style of presentation. Open courses, with delegates from different companies, are often tailored by asking delegates to take along material they can use to prepare a presentation directly connected with their work.

The cost of courses can be high (though costs vary considerably) but it can represent a good investment. Employers will often pay for managers to attend courses when there is sound reason.

Differences in approach mean that the best way to select a suitable course (from a shortlist of those covering the topics you want) is on the recommendation of someone who has already benefited from it. Presentation skills training is so widespread that you are likely to find a friend or colleague who has received training and can comment on the course.

Details of companies offering presentation skills training can be found in training directories and in management, training and personnel journals.

FURTHER READING

Bowman, L with Crofts, A (1991) *High Impact Business Presenta-tions. How to Speak like an Expert and Sound like a Statesman*, Business Books, London.

Bradbury, A J (1995) *Successful Presentation Skills*, Kogan Page, London.

Bunch, M (1989) *Speak with Confidence*, Kogan Page, London.

Denny, R (1994) *Speak for Yourself. Tested Techniques for Improving Your Presentation*, Kogan Page, London.

Dunckel, J and Parnham, E (1985) *The Business Guide to Effective Speaking*, Kogan Page, London.

Ehrenborg, J and Mattock, J (1993) *Powerful Presentations. 50 Original Ideas for Making a Real Impact*, Kogan Page, London.

Forsyth, P (1995) *Making Effective Presentations*, Sheldon Press, London.

Jay, A (1993) *Effective Presentation*, Pitman/The Institute of Management, London.

Kliem, R and Ludin, I S (1995) *Stand and Deliver: Fine Art of Presentation*, Gower, Aldershot.

Leech, T (1993) *How to Prepare, Stage, and Deliver Winning Presentations*, AMACOM, New York.

McKenzie, C (1993) *Successful Presentations*, Century Business, London.

Manchester Open Learning (1993) *Making Effective Presentations*, Kogan Page, London.

Martin, P J (1995) *More Effective Presentation*, Arlington Asso-ciates, Richmond.

Peel, M (1990) *Improving Your Communication Skills*, Kogan Page, London.

Peel, M (1995) *Successful Presentation in a Week*, Headway, London.

Robinson, N (1991) *Persuasive Business Presentations*, Mercury, London.

INDEX